ZEROING IN ON NUMBER AND OP

Key Ideas and Common Misconceptions, Grade

Linda Dacey and Anne Collins

Stenhouse Publishers
www.stenhouse.com

Copyright © 2011 by Linda Dacey and Anne Collins

Library of Congress Cataloging-in-Publication Data
Dacey, Linda Schulman, 1949-
  Zeroing in on number and operations : key ideas and common misconceptions, pre-K-K / Linda Dacey and Anne Collins.
      p. cm.
  Includes bibliographical references.
  ISBN 978-1-57110-858-6 (alk. paper)—ISBN 978-1-57110-894-4
  1. Mathematics—Study and teaching (Early childhood)
I. Collins, Anne, 1950– II. Title.
  QA135.6.D3344 2011
  372.7—dc22
                                                    2010041943

Cover design by Designboy Creative Group
Interior design and typesetting by MPS Limited, a Macmillan Company

Manufactured in the United States of America
17 16 15 14 13 12 11   9 8 7 6 5 4 3 2 1

Stenhouse Publishers
Portland, Maine

CONTENTS

The foundation for number and operations is built at the pre-K–K level. Too often, early childhood education does not place enough emphasis on the learning of mathematics, and when it does, the math instruction is not always taught in a developmentally appropriate manner. Young children should have the opportunity to explore mathematics through their natural play and through structured games and activities that meet their individual learning needs.

The National Governors Association and the Council of Chief State School Officers (2010) have recommended a curriculum that is focused with an emphasis on key topics. In prekindergarten and kindergarten, we focus on the key ideas that are essential for success at these levels:

- counting by rote, that is, saying the sequence of counting numbers in order
- counting rationally (with one-to-one correspondence and cardinality)
- subitizing, or recognizing sets
- counting by tens and ones
- making connections among representations of numbers
- comparing and ordering sets and numbers
- composing and decomposing numbers
- modeling addition as the joining of sets
- modeling subtraction as the separating of a set

The thirty modules in this flipchart are designed to engage all students in mathematical learning that develops conceptual understanding, addresses common misconceptions, and builds key ideas essential to future learning. The modules are research based and can be used to support a wide range of learners. Though Response to Intervention (RTI) is not often formalized at these levels, its philosophy of a well-integrated instructional system that addresses students' academic needs is embraced. These modules offer suggestions and resources for teachers seeking material for students identified as most likely to benefit from more support as well as enrichment activities and challenges for all students.

Following the recommendations of the National Council of Teachers of Mathematics (Fuson, Clements, and Beckmann 2010a, 2010b), we have organized these modules into three sections: Numbers, Relationships, and Addition and Subtraction. Each module begins with the identification of its **Mathematical Focus** and the **Potential Challenges and Misconceptions** associated with those ideas. **In the Classroom** then suggests instructional strategies and specific activities to implement with your students. **Meeting Individual Needs** offers ideas for adjusting the activities to reach a broader range of learners. Many activities are supported by a reproducible (located in the appendix), and **References/Further Reading** provides resources for enriching your knowledge of the topic and gathering more ideas.

Pre-K–K teachers work with children representing a wide range of developmental readiness. We have covered the full range of possibilities in these pages so you will be able to address multiple levels of learning, regardless of the specific ages of your students. Feel free to adjust the modules to best match your learners. You could modify the size of the numbers or the expectations for recording to make an activity more appropriate for your students.

REFERENCES/FURTHER READING

Fuson, Karen C., Douglas H. Clements, and Sybilla Beckmann. 2010a. *Focus in Kindergarten: Teaching with Curriculum Focal Points*. Reston, VA: National Council of Teachers of Mathematics.

———. 2010b. *Focus in Prekindergarten: Teaching with Curriculum Focal Points*. Reston, VA: National Council of Teachers of Mathematics.

National Governors Association (NGA) Center for Best Practices and Council of Chief State School Officers (CCSSO). 2010. Common Core State Standards. http://www.corestandards.org/the-standards.

One, Two, Three

Mathematical Focus

- Count to three (or four or five) using one-to-one correspondence.
- Count up to three (or four or five) objects to find how many.

Potential Challenges and Misconceptions

The number three can provide a challenge to our youngest students. Examples of one and two are commonplace in their lives (one head, one nose, two hands, two feet, two eyes), while examples of three are less common.

Though many young children can say the names of the numbers to three, or five, or even ten, this is only rote counting. Counting also includes the ability to say exactly one number name for each object counted. Even children who can count with this one-to-one correspondence may not realize that the last number they say is the number of items in the group. This aspect of counting is known as *cardinality*.

In the Classroom

One preschool teacher places three carpet samples in a row. She invites the two- and three-year-old children to count aloud with her as she points to the carpet pieces one at a time while saying, "One, two, three." She asks, "How many carpet pieces do we have?" Next she chooses three volunteers and has the first child stand on the first square and say, "One." The second and third children follow, saying "Two" and "Three." Then the teacher asks, "How many carpet pieces do we have? How many children are standing on these pieces of carpet?" Note that some learners may focus on the fact that there is one child on each piece of carpet and reply, "One," and others may need to count again to be sure. This is fine and just indicates that they need more opportunities to count to three. You can add more carpet pieces when the children are ready or when working with learners who are four or five years old.

Games also provide a good context for counting. For example, lead a game of "Teacher, May I?" and have the children take one to five baby or giant steps, counting aloud as they do so.

Meeting Individual Needs

The suggested activities are multisensory, which supports a variety of learners. Using a context with which children are familiar can also be beneficial. Several stories such as *Goldilocks and the Three Bears* and *The Three Little Pigs* bring attention to the number three. To provide children greater familiarity with three, read these stories aloud and have the children dramatize them.

It is important for children to develop one-to-one correspondence and cardinality with small numbers first. Once they master the numbers up to three, you can provide the challenge of working with greater numbers.

REFERENCES/FURTHER READING

Anderson, Ann, Jim Anderson, and Carolyn Thauberger. 2008. "Mathematics Learning and Teaching in the Early Years." In *Contemporary Perspectives on Mathematics in Early Childhood Education*, ed. Olivia N. Saracho and Bernard Spodek, 95–132. New York: Information Age.

Sarnecka, Barbara W., Valentina G. Kamenskaya, Yuko Yamana, Tamiko Ogura, and Yulia B. Yudovina. 2007. "From Grammatical Number to Exact Numbers: Early Meanings of 'One,' 'Two,' and 'Three' in English, Russian, and Japanese." *Cognitive Psychology* 55 (2): 136–68.

Mathematical Focus
- Say the names of the numbers in order.
- Connect the counting number sequence to the idea that each number is one more than the previous number.

Potential Challenges and Misconceptions

Memorizing the names of the counting numbers can be challenging for many children, especially if rote counting (saying the number names in order) is not incorporated into routines at home or if children are English language learners. One of the many functions of music is that it makes things easier to remember (Pound and Harrison 2003). When combined with finger actions or other dramatizations, songs can also support one-to-one correspondence and cardinality, or counting with meaning. Do not be surprised if children who are successful when they are singing experience difficulty when saying the number names without the support of a familiar song or rhyme.

In the Classroom

There are a variety of common songs and rhymes that involve the counting sequence. Two- and three-year-olds enjoy marching around while reciting or singing "One, Two, Buckle My Shoe," "Five Little Monkeys," and "This Old Man." You can also introduce songs for the children to dramatize. The process of doing so will help them make connections between number names and amounts. Consider the following two songs (sung to the tune of "Five Little Sea Shells," which can be heard at http://www.youtube.com/watch?v=42ilv3wc338) that are easily extended to five or ten. Counting backward is more challenging and generally reserved for older learners.

Try the following when introducing such songs:

- Have the children practice singing the words first.
- Have the children practice singing the song as they use their fingers to show the action.
- Ask for suggestions about how a small group could dramatize the song.
- Invite volunteers to dramatize the action as the remaining children continue to hold up the correct number of fingers as they sing the song.

Meeting Individual Needs

You can easily adapt these songs to meet a variety of interests. Racing cars may be more engaging than twinkling stars. You can also make connections to your classroom areas, for example, by changing "Ten in the Bed" to "Ten on the Rug." You can start or end songs at three, five, or ten to meet different levels of readiness. Encourage children who speak languages other than English to teach the class songs in their languages.

REFERENCE/FURTHER READING

Pound, Linda, and Chris Harrison. 2003. *Supporting Musical Development in the Early Years*. Buckingham, UK: Open University Press.

One little doggie sitting on a chair.
One more doggie comes to be there.
Two little doggies sitting on chairs.
One more doggie comes to be there.
Three little doggies sitting on chairs.
Don't you wish that you could be there?

Three twinkling stars lighting up the sky.
One gets covered by a cloud coming by.
Two twinkling stars lighting up the sky.
One gets covered by a cloud coming by.
One twinkling star lighting up the sky.
The cloud comes by and then there are none.

Mathematical Focus

- Connect number names, symbols, and quantities up to five.
- Recognize amounts of one through five without counting (subitize).

Potential Challenges and Misconceptions

Number sense is more than counting. Over time, children gain the ability to recognize the number of objects in a small group without even counting them. With many opportunities to count, two- and three-year-olds may recognize a group of one, two, or three items. Four- and five-year-olds can learn to recognize greater numbers as well, especially if they are arranged in a familiar pattern, such as the way five is represented on dice. This ability is known as *subitizing*.

Some children only subitize the numbers one and two, which will lead to later difficulties. Knowing a number such as five well allows it to serve as a benchmark, that is, a number to which other numbers can be compared, an idea critical to ordering numbers. Children of ages four and five can use their recognition of the number five to build a sense of the numbers six through ten.

In the Classroom

Many children have a visual image of five, as they know they have five fingers on each hand. One preschool teacher uses finger puppets to connect the process of counting to five to that of finding the total quantity of five. As the teacher places each puppet on a child's hand, the child counts it aloud. When asked how many puppets there are in all, many children count again from one, rather than just reply, "Five." This teacher makes a point to reinforce the notion of cardinality by saying, "Yes, the last number you said tells us there are five puppets. Can you wiggle all puppets at once?"

Place sticky dots on paper plates to provide a quick representation of numbers. Stick one on a plate, two on another, and so forth. You can ask younger prekindergarten children to place a counter on each dot to count the dots; to make a set of counters on another plate to match the number of dots on a given plate; or to recognize the plates for one to three when flashed quickly. Older pre-K and K learners can match different arrangements of the same number of dots; recognize sets of four and five; and match the number of dots to number symbols.

Five-frames offer a more structured organization of the numbers one through five. An empty frame can be used as a frame upon which children can build numbers or as a model for zero. Make copies of the *Five-Frames* reproducible on page A1 in the appendix. Cut out the frames and laminate them. The frames can be used in ways similar to the dot plates, but they better support understanding of relationships among numbers. For example, they can help learners recognize that four is one less than five (see figure).

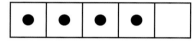

Meeting Individual Needs

The symbol for two is often confused with the symbol for five. There are a variety of ways to involve kinesthetic learning in the recognition of symbols that can help children better differentiate these numbers. Examples include pretending to write large symbols in the air and tracing sandpaper symbols with their fingers.

REFERENCE/FURTHER READING

Novakowski, Janice. 2007. "Developing 'Five-ness' in Kindergarten." *Teaching Children Mathematics* 14 (4): 226–31.

Counting Routines

Mathematical Focus
- Count by rote.
- Count rationally.

Potential Challenges and Misconceptions

Counting is much more complex than many adults realize. Children must know the correct sequence of the number names; count one and only one object for each number name they say; know that the last number they say identifies the number of objects in the group (cardinality); know that the cardinality of a group does not change if the objects are rearranged (stability); and make connections between number names, quantities, and symbols.

Too often adults assume that children who exhibit these abilities with numbers less than five (or ten) will also do so with greater numbers. This is often not the case. It takes time and considerable practice for these concepts and skills to develop. We must support routines that involve counting and take advantage of the many opportunities available to integrate number activities throughout the day.

In the Classroom

There are many opportunities for children to practice counting during daily activities, for example, climbing up or down stairs, taking attendance, passing out paintbrushes, and keeping track of the number of questions allowed to be asked at morning meetings. You can also create a variety of routines that support both rote counting and counting with meaning (rational counting). For example:

- *Number Tray*: Each day, place some counters on a lunch tray. Sometime during the day, each child should count to find the quantity on the tray. Depending on ability, the child should then either whisper his or her answer to you or write the number on a slip of paper and hand it to you.
- *Estimate It*: When outside, ask questions such as *How many steps do you think it is to that tree?* Then have the children count each step as they walk to the tree.

- *Clothes Counts*: While sitting in the rug area, ask, *How many shoes (buttons, stripes, pockets) are you wearing today?* After each child counts to decide, have three children demonstrate their counts.
- *Tower Fall*: Have children place one block on top of another, counting as they do so, until the stack falls down.
- *Flash*: Cover a plate of counters with a cloth. Quickly remove and replace the cloth. Ask the children to estimate how many counters they saw. Then choose a volunteer to count to check.

Meeting Individual Needs

English language learners may be able to count to greater numbers in their languages but lack knowledge of the number sequence in English. While they learn the new number names, have these children occasionally count in their languages as well. While they do so, you can check their understanding of one-to-one correspondence, cardinality, and stability. Also, encourage choral counting so that the voices of others can prompt ELLs to remember the correct names and sequence.

REFERENCES/FURTHER READING

Galizio, Carolyn, Julia Stoll, and Pamela Hutchins. 2009. "'We Need a Way to Get to the Other Side!': Exploring the Possibilities for Learning in Natural Spaces." *Young Children* 64 (4): 42–48.

Kalifatidou, Eleftheria R. 2008. "Design of Activities on Numerical Representations Based on Cognitive Research." *Teaching Children Mathematics* 14 (6): 355–60.

Mathematical Focus

- Relate counting and cardinality.
- Recognize and use number names.
- Realize that the number of a set does not change when the items are rearranged (stability).

Potential Challenges and Misconceptions

Two- and three-year-old children love to recite the number names, but most lack understanding of their meaning. Sometimes they count in the correct sequence and other times they do not. Children often continue saying the number names after all the objects have been counted. At a restaurant, a two-year-old might be given four crayons and a placemat to color. She might say, "Watch me count these," and count from one to ten, pointing to various crayons as she does so, stopping only because ten is the last number name she knows.

Her four-year-old brother might look over and without counting say, "No, there are four." Yet this same boy might be given seven animal crackers, skip one while he counts them, and report that he has six. Both of these children are developing their number sense as they continue to count sets and develop facility with all aspects of counting.

In the Classroom

I Spy is a game in which young children are challenged to identify the mystery set that is described. An adult begins by putting different amounts of objects on various trays and placing the trays around the room in visible locations. The objects may include a variety of counters, including but not limited to small cars, balls, blocks, crayons, pencils, and large buttons.

For two- and three-year-olds, the game begins with the teacher choosing from one to three objects. The teacher might say, "I spy a set of two. Who can tell me what is in the set I see?"

The children look around a small area of the room to see if they can identify a set of two. A child might say, "I see two balls."

The teacher continues by stating, "I spy a set of three. Who can tell me what is in the set I see?"

Older children can assume the role of teacher, saying, "I spy a set of _____. Who can tell me what is in the set I see?"

To assess whether children understand that rearranging the objects does not change their quantity, move the objects on the tray just "spied" and provide the same number clue. Note those children who understand the stability of numbers and have the memory skills to identify the set without counting.

Meeting Individual Needs

You can individualize the number of objects included in the game *I Spy* for various children. Give those children who can identify only a set of up to three items the time they need to develop their confidence before increasing the number of objects, regardless of their age.

REFERENCE/FURTHER READING

Van de Walle, John A., Karen S. Karp, and Jennifer M. Bay-Williams. 2010. *Elementary and Middle School Mathematics: Teaching Developmentally.* 7th ed. New York: Pearson Education.

Which One?

Mathematical Focus

- Count objects that are immovable.
- Use the process of elimination.

Potential Challenges and Misconceptions

It is a challenge for children to keep track of items they are counting. They may skip an item or count it more than once. When they use counters, young students can move each one off to one side after counting it. But keeping track visually, when they cannot move objects, is more difficult. Some children may want to make a mark on each item they count in a picture to help them keep track.

In the Classroom

Using clues to identify the correct picture gives children opportunities to count objects that cannot be moved. The *Find It* reproducible on page A2 in the appendix provides pictures for you to copy. The pictures can be used with a wide variety of learners, so you may want to copy them on heavy stock and use them at different times during the year. For example:

- With a small group of two- and three-year-old children, show them just one of the pictures in each row at a time and ask them counting questions. For instance, show a picture of one of the plants and ask, *How many flowers does this plant have? How many leaves does this plant have? How many stripes do you see on the pot?* Help the children count each of the items you specify.

- Show some three-year-olds and most four-year-olds all three of the pictures of the plants and ask, *What is the same about these plants? What is different?* Then say, *I have a plant that has exactly three leaves. Which picture shows this plant?* Help the children check the number of leaves on each plant. Similarly, you could identify this same plant with the clue *I have a plant with one flower* or *I have a plant in a pot with two dark stripes.* You can use the pictures of houses and monsters in the same manner.

- For learners ready for a greater challenge, you can provide two clues they must use to identify a plant. For example, tell the children that they are going to use clues to find the picture of

Mr. Chen's plant. Give the first clue, *Mr. Chen's plant has four leaves*, and record a 4 on chart paper or the board. Help the children check each picture and recognize that they can eliminate one of the pictures. Then follow the same process for the final clue: *Mr. Chen's plant has one flower.* Once the children have identified the correct plant, have the children look at it while you review the clues: *four leaves, one flower.* Say, *This picture meets all of the clues.*

For the house and the monster pictures, you can provide students one clue to identify the correct picture or give them the following sets of clues.

In which house does Krista live?	Which monster did Rusty draw?
• Her house has five windows. • Her house has two trees in front of it.	• His monster has three eyes. • His monster has five legs. • His monster has two hairs.

Meeting Individual Needs

To help children keep track of pictures they have eliminated, cut out the pictures in each row so that students can turn them over when they don't match a clue. Alternatively, make copies of the reproducible on copy paper and have children cross off any picture that does not meet a clue.

Make the clues more complex to offer a greater challenge. For example, change *There are four leaves* to *There are two more leaves than flowers.*

REFERENCE/FURTHER READING

Sarama, Julie, and Douglas H. Clements. 2007. "Early Math: How Children Problem Solve: Helping Children Use Problem-Solving Strategies in the Classroom." *Early Childhood Today* 21 (7): 16–19.

Mathematical Focus

- Anchor numbers to five and ten.
- Count on from five.
- Recognize numbers represented on a ten-frame.

Potential Challenges and Misconceptions

The likelihood that children will make counting errors increases with greater quantities. As the number of items to be counted increases, children might skip a number name, neglect an object, or count an item more than once. Arrangement also matters. For example, it is easier to count objects in a row than when they appear in a random organization. Placing items in groups of five or ten helps learners keep track of what they are counting.

Organizing numbers in five-frames (see "All About Five") helps students count with accuracy and relate numbers to the benchmark number five. Two rows of five squares create a ten-frame, which is introduced in this activity.

In the Classroom

Model counting a group of six counters by placing the first five counters in an empty five-frame (see the *Five-Frames* reproducible on page A1 in the appendix) and one more counter beside the frame, as shown (see figure). Then ask the children to do the same. Using the five-frame helps children see six as one more than five. Have children tell the number of counters and match the set to the number symbol. Follow the same procedure for the numbers seven through nine.

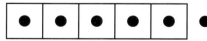

Children can also relate these numbers to their fingers; that is, they can show five on one hand and one to four more on the other hand. Over time, some children will be able to recognize the five and *count on*, saying, "six, seven, eight, nine."

Kindergarten students can be introduced to the ten-frames, which are 2-by-5 arrays used to model the numbers one through ten in a way that anchors them to five and ten. Make copies of the *Ten-Frames* reproducible on pages A3–A6 in the appendix on heavy stock, cut out the frames, and give a set to each child. The frame for eight, for example, provides a visual model of eight as three more than five and two less than ten (see figure). This visual model supports eventual connections to $5 + 3 = 8$ and $10 - 2 = 8$. Once you've had students build the numbers in order, call out numbers in a random sequence and have the children build them on empty frames.

These frames can be used in a variety of ways. For example:

- Have children arrange the frames in order, with or without your support, and then ask them to identify frames as you call out random numbers.
- Give pairs of children two sets (or partial sets) of ten-frames and have the children match the frames that show the same numbers.
- Have children work in pairs with one set of frames organized in order. One child closes his or her eyes while the other removes one of the frames. The first child then identifies the one that is missing.
- Hold up a frame and have the children tell the number they see.

Meeting Individual Needs

While there is great value in using the frames, children still need many opportunities to count objects without using these tools. Have children count objects in lines, arrays, circles, and then random arrangements to assess their ability to keep track. Make a copy of the *Counting Assessment Form* reproducible on page A7 in the appendix and note each child's ability to work with different numbers. Make and complete another copy later in the year to document growth over time.

REFERENCE/FURTHER READING

Losq, Christine. 2005. "Number Concepts and Special Needs Students: The Power of Ten-Frame Tiles." *Teaching Children Mathematics* 11 (6): 310–15.

Picture Cards

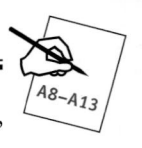

Mathematical Focus
- Recognize the quantities in sets.
- Recognize numerals.
- Match sets to corresponding numerals.

Potential Challenges and Misconceptions

Children can recite the number names before they can associate them with their symbols. To develop number sense, children must connect these symbols with their related number names and quantities. These connections can also deepen children's understanding of cardinality. It takes significant time and practice for children to make the important links among these representations. Unfortunately, we often do not devote enough time to this significant learning goal, and young children who do not make these associations will experience difficulties.

Children as young as two should be exposed to the symbols for the numbers up to three. By the end of prekindergarten, children are expected to read numerals to ten, and kindergarten children continue this work through nineteen. Note that *numerals*, rather than *numbers*, is the correct term for the written symbols, though we do not require this distinction with young children.

In the Classroom

Young children can engage in a variety of activities that develop and solidify understanding of number symbols (numerals), cardinality, and, if ready, written number names. *Matching Puzzle Pieces* is one activity that engages children as young as two, but more often three-year-olds; see the *Number Puzzles* reproducible on pages A8–A11 in the appendix for a sample set of puzzle pieces. Two- and three-year-olds work with a teacher, while older children can work individually. Players spread the pieces out in front of them and then match the numeral pieces with their associated quantities, making a pile of the completed pairs of puzzle pieces.

In one classroom, Manny, a four-year-old, tells his partner, "One, two, three, four. I have four trains, and that is four," as he points to the puzzle piece with the numeral 4. Yasmine, who is three years old, randomly finds two puzzle pieces and then counts, "One, two, three. I have three stars." Her teacher partner observes that Yasmine uses trial and error to find two pieces that fit correctly and pays little attention to the numeral. The teacher draws Yasmine's attention to the numeral, asking, "What does this mean?"

Number Concentration is an activity designed for pairs; game cards are provided in the *Concentration Cards* reproducible on pages A12 and A13 in the appendix. Children ages two and three play with a teacher and may only begin with the cards from one through three. Older learners can play together with adult supervision and could begin with the cards for one though five or six. As with all new activities, begin by modeling the game for the children. Place the game cards faceup in an array. One child selects two cards that he thinks match and counts to check. If the cards do not match, the student returns the cards and the next child (or the teacher partner) takes a turn. The game continues until the players have paired all the cards. At these ages, the activity should not be competitive. Over time, note those numbers for which students recognize a set (subitize) and those for which the children need to count.

Meeting Individual Needs

Children who do not exhibit confidence with their counting or with recognizing that the last number they say is the number of items in the set will benefit from repeated opportunities to play these games. Do not rush the children through these activities, but rather allow them to play for understanding. For children who are ready for more of a challenge, include cards with numbers up to seven or even ten.

For an even greater challenge when playing *Number Concentration*, have children place the array of cards facedown to develop memory as well as number recognition.

REFERENCE/FURTHER READING
Clements, Douglas H. 1999. "Subitizing: What Is It? Why Teach It?" *Teaching Children Mathematics* 5 (7): 400–405.

Focus on Numerals

Mathematical Focus

- Read number symbols (numerals) to ten (or nineteen).
- Connect numerals to number names.
- Write numerals.

Potential Challenges and Misconceptions

Recognizing or reading number symbols is part of learning to count. Just as young learners need to practice saying the sequence of numbers to commit it to memory, they also need to practice reading and writing numerals. This is more challenging than adults might realize, as some numerals—for example, 4s—do not always look the same.

Reading numerals is easier than writing them, and some numerals are easier to write than others. For example, 1 is easier to write than 8. Children are more likely to reverse some numerals than others, such as 3, perhaps confusing it with the letter *E*. The symbols 2 and 5 as well as 6 and 9 may cause confusion because of their similarities. Reversals are common in the teen numbers because children often write them as they hear them; that is, they might write *31* for thirteen. Since 1 is an easy symbol to record, writing the teen numbers requires relatively less muscle control than writing other two-digit numbers.

In the Classroom

The *Number Cards* reproducible on pages A14–A17 in the appendix provides cards with the numerals 1–19. Use as many of the cards as appropriate, depending on your students' readiness levels. Make copies on heavy stock, and laminate them if possible, as you can use the cards in a variety of activities. For example:

- Distribute the cards randomly and have the children, one at a time, hang them up on a clothesline or place them on a chalk tray in order. Initially, prompt the children by saying, "Who has 1? Who has 2?" Later have the children try to complete the activity without prompting.
- Bring three sets of the cards outside or to the gym and place them in three piles about 40 feet away from the children. As you call the numbers aloud, in order, three teams of children retrieve the cards, one at a time in relay-type fashion, and place them in a row on the ground or floor by their teams.

- Hang up the number cards randomly and challenge the children to put them in order.

Greg Nelson (2007) suggests that teachers cut out pictures of numerals from magazines or newspapers or type them using different type sizes and fonts and print them out. Have the children sort the numerals, placing those representing the same number together.

Children may be interested in making a number "necklace." Cut blank file cards in half and punch two holes at the top of each one. Have the children write numerals on the cards and weave them together in order with pieces of string or long shoelaces that can then be tied behind the children's necks. Have adult volunteers make the numerals for the youngest children, combining them with matching pictures of objects.

Meeting Individual Needs

These activities can involve the numerals 1–3, 1–5, 1–10, or 1–19, depending on students' readiness. Though the goal for prekindergarten children is to write a few of the numerals from 1 through 10 and for kindergartners to write the numerals from 1 through 19, children's ability to write numbers varies widely at these levels. Using their fingers to trace over numbers that you have "written" in a plate of sand or cornmeal can help children build muscle memory. Some learners may need additional opportunities to trace numbers using models with arrows that indicate the correct sequence of motions.

REFERENCE/FURTHER READING

Nelson, Greg. 2007. *Math at Their Own Pace: Child-Directed Activities for Developing Early Number Sense.* St. Paul, MN: Redleaf.

Mathematical Focus

- Connect representations of numbers.

Potential Challenges and Misconceptions

Teachers need to ensure that children see numbers represented in a variety of ways (counters, drawings, tally marks, five- or ten-frames, words, symbols) and connect them to everyday examples. One teacher makes a particular effort to ponder aloud about numbers. For example, one day she says, "I was just thinking about the number eight. Both a spider and an octopus have eight legs." Such connections to the real world help children avoid the misconception that learning math is just for school.

Lesh, Post, and Behr (1987) identify five representations for concepts: pictures, manipulative models, real-world situations, oral language, and written symbols. Their diagram of these representational forms emphasizes the many connections among them (see figure).

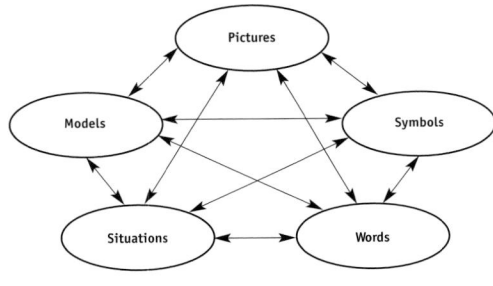

In the Classroom

One prekindergarten teacher reads *Ten Black Dots* (Crews 1985) with her students. The second time she reads it, she asks them to anticipate the number of dots there will be on the next page. A kindergarten teacher investigates *Anno's Counting Book* (Anno 1986) with his students. Together they talk about how the pictures change. They discover that the number of houses, trees, children, and so forth is the same within a two-page spread and that the number increases by one each time they turn the page. He has a basket full of counting books in the classroom library, and for a couple of weeks, he chooses a different one each day to read with the children. Throughout the week, the chosen books are displayed prominently on a table so that the children can revisit them during math workshop time.

With adult support, children can create their own number books with one page for each number. It is best to prepare the books ahead of time. Take the appropriate number (depending on the readiness of each child) of 8.5 by 11 inch pieces of paper and

fold the stack to make pages that are 8.5 by 5.5. Staple the sheets together along the outside of the folded edge. Over the course of a week, the children can make a page for each number, starting at one. See the figure for an example of a page made by a kindergarten student. Lucas drew five sets of three, including writing the number name and the numeral three times each. Not surprisingly, he reversed the numeral. His older sister taught him how to write his name in cursive, and as this was an artistic project, he signed the page with his first name in cursive (see the rectangular area near the bottom of the page).

Meeting Individual Needs

You can vary your expectations for the children's number books according to their readiness. Students can include the numbers 1–3, 1–5, or 1–10, or they can focus on the teen numbers. You can also adjust the complexity of their work, perhaps asking them to show only one representation of each number or to illustrate the numbers in a variety of ways. Some kindergarten children may want to include expressions equal to the numbers. Kinesthetic learners may want to include shapes cut from sandpaper so that they can feel the quantity represented.

REFERENCES/FURTHER READING

Anno, Mitsumasa. 1986. *Anno's Counting Book*. New York: HarperCollins.
Crews, Donald. 1985. *Ten Black Dots*. New York: Greenwillow.
Lesh, Richard, Thomas Post, and Merlyn Behr. 1987. "Representations and Translations Among Representations in Mathematics Learning and Problem Solving." In *Problems of Representation in the Teaching and Learning of Mathematics*, ed. Claude Janvier, 33–40. Hillsdale, NJ: Erlbaum.

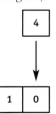

Mathematical Focus

- Count by rote to nineteen.
- Connect names, symbols, and quantities for the teen numbers.
- Recognize the teen numbers as being composed of ten and some more.

Potential Challenges and Misconceptions

There is a good reason that children have trouble with the teen numbers. The names for these numbers are irregular. Unlike our other two-digit numbers, the ones are said before the tens; for example, we say "sixteen" instead of "teensix." The names for *eleven* and *twelve* don't even suggest that there are two parts to the numbers. Though familiar names for the ones can be heard in *fourteen* and *sixteen* through *nineteen*, *thirteen* and *fifteen* both transform the names *three* and *five*. These irregularities make it difficult for young learners to remember the sequence of the number names and to match names and quantities with correct symbols. Though some three-year-olds can say the teen numbers in order by rote and some four-year-olds can correctly count up to fifteen objects placed in a row, it is not until kindergarten that children explore the notion that a teen number is made up of one ten and some more ones.

In the Classroom

Though children may struggle with the teen numbers, it is important not to avoid them. When we offer children challenges, they are able to develop more complex ideas. One teacher tells a story about a family going out to dinner together. There are Grandpa and Grandma Garcia, Papa and Nana Rogers, Mom, Dad, Carlos, Maria, Krista, and Manny. Using copies of the blank ten-frame on page A3 in the appendix, she asks the children to place a counter in the frame for each member of the family. They agree that there will be ten people at the family dinner.

The teacher then dramatizes the mother of the family getting a call from Uncle Mac. "Hello, Uncle Mac," she says. "We're having a family dinner tonight. Do you want to join us?" She says good-bye and ponders, "Hmm, if Uncle Mac comes, how many people will that be?" Some children know that eleven is one more than ten; others put a chip to the side of the ten-frame and count from one to eleven (see figure). The teacher reinforces the number by saying, "Yes, that's right, we will have ten and one more, or eleven people, at the family dinner."

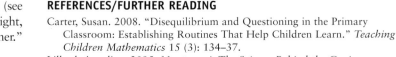

Over time the story gets longer and longer, until finally there are nineteen people at the dinner. The day the teacher knows that the story will get to fifteen, she introduces the idea of using two empty ten-frames, one to show the counters for the family of ten and one to organize the other counters. The next figure shows the number seventeen organized in this way. As the children get to know the story better, they enjoy dramatizing the phone calls and using names from their families.

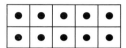

Children need many opportunities to count groups with between eleven and nineteen objects and to connect the amounts with the correct symbols. You can set up a teen corner and choose a number to focus on each day. Have the children link cubes, bundle sticks, and place counters in small plastic containers to experience making a ten as they form the number represented by that day's symbol.

Meeting Individual Needs

Some children may be ready to match the symbols for the teen numbers with corresponding sets, and still others may be ready to write the numerals themselves. Encourage them to do so. Others will benefit from using the cards in the *Teen Cards* reproducible on page A18 in the appendix. Cut out the cards, adapted from more extensive Montessori materials, and give each child a set. To form the number 14, for example, a child should place the 4 card over the 0 in the 10 card (see figure).

4

↓

1 0

REFERENCES/FURTHER READING

Carter, Susan. 2008. "Disequilibrium and Questioning in the Primary Classroom: Establishing Routines That Help Children Learn." *Teaching Children Mathematics* 15 (3): 134–37.

Lillard, Angeline. 2005. *Montessori: The Science Behind the Genius.* New York: Oxford University Press.

Mathematical Focus

- Say the number names in sequence from one to one hundred.
- Say the number names for the decades from ten to one hundred.
- Connect the number names to the number symbols.

Potential Challenges and Misconceptions

In most Asian languages, the number names help children recognize the pattern of the count in two-digit numbers. The names follow the pattern without exception. The number of tens is said, followed by the number of ones. If our language did the same, we would have number names such as *one ten–five* and *three tens–six*. Our number names do not make the pattern explicit. The suffix *-ty* is used instead of *ten*. *Twenty* does not sound like *two* and *thirty* does not sound like *three*. Though you can recognize *four* in *forty*, *five* and *fifty* do not sound the same. It is not until the sixties, seventies, eighties, and nineties that the names for the number of tens match our names for ones consistently.

Most two- and three-year-olds enjoy reciting the number names, and although they tend to include some invented names or recite the numbers out of order, they are developing the sense that the numbers continue, which is an important mathematical idea. Most four- and five-year-olds are proud of their ability to count by rote, though they, too, make errors as their range increases. It is not uncommon to hear kindergarten children say "twenty-ten" after "twenty-nine" as they follow the ones pattern that they know. Others may say "twenty-niiiine," dragging out the sound of *nine* as they try to think of the name for the next decade. When they remember *thirty* on their own or through prompting, they then return to a quicker pace.

In the Classroom

Counting by tens to one hundred can be exciting, and it is not unusual to hear a child say, "I can count by tens; want to hear me?" It is important to try to find the time to listen each time a child wants to count. Though it is a rote counting sequence, children gain the sense that they are counting by a number other than ones when they

- flash their ten fingers each time they say one of the decade names (*ten, twenty, thirty*, etc.) or
- make a big, full circle with their arms as they say each decade name.

Doing such activities during transition times can release energy and provide the practice young students need.

In grades one and two, we suggest that students write the symbols for the numbers one to one hundred on adding machine tape so that the numbers are listed one beneath the other. The vertical arrangement helps students see the patterns in both the ones and the tens columns. For younger children, the National Council of Teachers of Mathematics (Fuson, Clements, and Beckmann 2010) suggests showing the numbers in each group of ten in separate columns. One kindergarten teacher makes bookmark-type cards containing these lists and calls them *number sticks*. She laminates them, and when introducing them to a small group, she gives each child a set, placed in order. She also makes a large display of the sticks that she hangs in the classroom.

To make your own cards, copy the *Number Sticks* reproducible on pages A19 and A20 in the appendix. When using the sticks, have the children

- build up slowly to 100, beginning, perhaps, with the number sticks for 1 to 30;
- practice counting by tens while pointing to the last number in each column;
- talk about the patterns they see;
- count by ones as they touch each corresponding symbol;
- answer questions such as *Where is the number twenty-eight? In which stick will we find the number seventy-four?*;
- put the sticks in order.

Meeting Individual Needs

Recognizing the number symbols in order is very different from recognizing them in a random arrangement. As Dacey and Eston (1999) suggest, show students a collection of random numbers and ask children to tell you which ones they know. The *Number Search* reproducible on page A21 in the appendix shows a sample arrangement. Give a copy to a kindergarten child and say, "Point to the numbers you know and tell me their names." Make a copy for yourself as well, so you can mark each number the child identifies correctly or note any misidentifications. It's worth repeating this activity two or three times a year to note growth over time.

REFERENCES/FURTHER READING

Dacey, Linda S., and Rebeka Eston. 1999. *Growing Mathematical Ideas in Kindergarten*. Sausalito, CA: Math Solutions.

Fuson, Karen C., Douglas H. Clements, and Sybilla Beckmann. 2010. *Focus in Kindergarten: Teaching with Curriculum Focal Points*. Reston, VA: National Council of Teachers of Mathematics.

Playing with Math

Mathematical Focus
- Compare the quantities of groups.
- Use the terms *more*, *less*, and *the same*.
- Make comparisons in everyday life.

Potential Challenges and Misconceptions

More is a word that most children use early. A two-year-old may emphatically say, "More!" after eating a snack or listening to a story. This statement is not connected to counting but, rather, a sense of wanting more of the same. Young children are usually comparing sets perceptually when they query, "Why does he have more?" They are typically not ready for the challenge of using counting or matching to compare sets. Two- and three-year-olds need many opportunities to compare groups with five or fewer items to reinforce the connections among the counting sequence and which is more. Most four- and five-year-olds can use counting or one-to-one correspondence to compare sets up to five, but they may still be challenged by sets of greater quantities. Play provides many natural opportunities for making comparisons.

In the Classroom

At the dress-up area you may hear, "You have more necklaces. I want more." You might hear a similar conversation about the number of blocks being used in the building area of the room. Initially, children make such comparisons perceptually by noting the density of the objects in a group or the length of the objects in a row. You can also ask questions to solicit their initial opinions about the relationship between two sets. Follow these questions with *Why do you think so?* to give children the chance to reflect on their perceptual decisions and make them more explicit. You can also purposely include activities and materials that encourage comparisons. For example:

- Put a set of teacups and saucers in the dramatic play area, but remove one of the saucers. Observe how different children react to the missing saucer. In one preschool classroom, Kira announces that another saucer is needed. Lamont says it doesn't matter and they can use the cup without the saucer. Jani suggests that they just put a cup away. What's important is that they all noticed the difference in quantity.
- Play musical chairs with a small group of children while the other children watch. For the first round, have the same number of chairs and children so that each child can be successful in finding a chair when you stop the music. Remove one chair each time a new round begins. At the end and beginning of each round ask, *Were there more children or chairs?* or *Are there fewer children or chairs?*
- *Squirrels and Trees* is a game similar to musical chairs that you can play outside, as no equipment is needed. Have children volunteer to be trees. They stand still with their arms out to represent branches while the same number of volunteers run around, pretending to be squirrels. When you call, "Go to your trees!" each squirrel must find an empty tree. Again start with the same number of trees as squirrels, and then decrease the number of trees by one each time. Most children find the game exciting and are attentive to the process.
- Tug-of-war requires two teams to hold onto either side of a long piece of cloth to try to force the other team to cross the middle line. The game emphasizes the importance of having players with the same strength on each side. Young children interpret this as meaning the same number of players on each side. One teacher brings the children to a matted area and purposely sets up a game with, for instance, six players on one side and two on the other. As the two players are easily pulled to the other team's side, they protest, "This isn't fair!" The teacher then helps them decide how to make sure there is the same number of players on each team.

Meeting Individual Needs

Children with limited mobility can often still play *Squirrels and Trees* and musical chairs if they stay near a tree or chair, and those in wheelchairs sometimes win the tree game.

Occasionally, there is a child who does not make intuitive comparisons of quantity. Baroody was one of the first researchers to suggest that "a child unable to use 'more' in this intuitive manner is at considerable educational risk" (1987, 29). Such a child needs many opportunities to compare groups with an obvious difference in quantity. For example, show a group of two blocks and a group of twelve blocks. Say, *Which group of blocks would you like to use to build a house? Why?*

REFERENCE/FURTHER READING

Baroody, Arthur J. 1987. *Children's Mathematical Thinking: A Developmental Framework for Preschool, Primary, and Special Education Teachers.* New York: Teachers College Press.

Comparing with Egg Cartons

Mathematical Focus

- Use one-to-one correspondence to determine which set is greater.
- Use the terms *more*, *less*, and *the same*.

Potential Challenges and Misconceptions

Researchers make a variety of claims about the ability of infants and animals to discriminate among the numerosity of sets (Pound 2008). Most agree, however, that we have underestimated the ability to recognize which of two sets is greater when each contains a small number of items. Yet this intuitive attention to the greater set may be the reason that children are not likely to use the comparative term *less*. Teachers should make a particular effort to emphasize use of this word.

It is also important for young learners to develop techniques for making comparisons that do not rely solely on intuition and that allow for making discriminations between sets that are close in number.

In the Classroom

Egg cartons are inexpensive and can provide a way to model the use of one-to-one correspondence to make comparisons. They also help children organize counters in rows, with exactly one item above another, increasing the likelihood of success.

One preschool teacher demonstrates the use of a carton with a small group of children. She shows them a set of three blue counters and a set of four red counters. She has arranged the groups so that the objects within a set overlap, making their numerosity less readily apparent. She says, "Hmm, I wonder if there are more blue counters or red counters." Then she places the blue counters in the first row of the carton while explaining, "I am going to start here [pointing to the left-most side of the top row] and put one counter in each place. I am not going to skip any places. I am only going to use the top row." She then repeats with the red counters, putting them in the second row, and asks the children to decide whether there are more blue counters or red counters and to tell how they know (see figure). The students give a variety of reasons for their responses, including "Because it's longer," "I can see there are more," and "The blues stop first."

Next she asks, "Which number is less, three or four?"

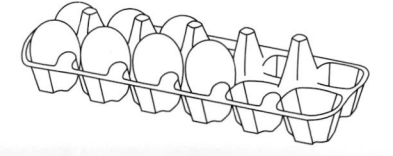

The teacher then demonstrates other examples, including ones with equal sets. She will repeat the activity over many days and give each child an individual egg carton to use.

While younger children need to work directly with an adult, four- and five-year-olds can work more independently. One kindergarten classroom has a learning center with egg cartons and a variety of sets placed in plastic bags. The goal is for the children to compare two sets, decide the numerical relationship between them, and record their findings. Each bag is labeled with a letter and contains one to six objects. The teacher helps the children understand the directions, and there is a sign posted that illustrates the relationships of more, less, and the same along with the corresponding words. Children choose two bags randomly and compare their amounts. The children continue until they can find a combination for each comparison listed on the recording sheet. The *Compare It* reproducible on page A22 in the appendix is an example of such a sheet.

Meeting Individual Needs

You can tape two egg cartons together end-to-end to allow students to compare greater numbers. Half-dozen cartons (or cartons cut in half) can be used to compare the numbers one through three. Examples that relate sets of different colors or shapes are easier for children to distinguish. Eventually, children should compare the quantity of sets regardless of their composition, though some children may need more time without this distraction.

REFERENCE/FURTHER READING

Pound, Linda. 2008. *Thinking and Learning About Mathematics in the Early Years*. New York: Routledge.

Mathematical Focus

- Create equivalent sets.
- Count to confirm that sets are equivalent.

Potential Challenges and Misconceptions

Ginsberg and Ertle remind us that "indeed, simple mathematical 'skills' are far more conceptual than we often realize" (2008, 54). While we may think it is a simple skill to match a knife with every fork, such a task underpins a conceptual model for the notion of equality, an idea that permeates the mathematics curriculum at all levels. Young children use matching to establish equality. This one-to-one correspondence between one object and another object is different from the correspondence between an object and a number name that is emphasized in counting and requires separate attention.

As children progress in school, they form many misconceptions about what the equal sign means. Too often, they interpret it as *find the answer and write it in the next space*. It is important that even our youngest students begin to understand that *equal to* is a relationship that indicates that two groups or expressions have the same amount or value.

In the Classroom

Children intuitively match objects to objects at a young age. *One for you and one for me* is a familiar phrase, and most children are quick to point it out when the equality is not maintained. They may gather a sock for each foot and a mitten for each hand. Children need many opportunities to make these ideas more explicit. The youngest learners can pursue these activities with one to three objects and then up to five. By the end of kindergarten, children should be able to work with sets of up to ten items. Possible activities include the following:

- *Felt Board Match:* Demonstrate matching objects on the felt board. For example, you could match flowers to stems, dogs to bones, or doors to houses. Then invite the children to help with the matching process. Make sure each task is summarized with a statement using *equal to* or *the same number as*, introducing both phrases during the course of the activity.
- *Hide and Seek Partners:* Place some same-size containers in the rug area and hide the same number of lids nearby. Have the children count (or subitize) to find the number of containers and then ask, "How many lids do we need?" Then send the children to seek the lids hidden in the designated area. When the lids are found, invite volunteers to match them to the containers and confirm that there is the same number of lids as containers. Repeat with other commonly matched items.

- *Back-to-Back:* Give two children several counters and have them sit back-to-back. Call out a number and have each child make a group of that amount. Then have the children check that the sets are equal by matching their items.
- *Match Me:* You or a child makes a set and then the other children make a set with the same quantity. With younger children, have them match the set, one counter at a time, to make an equivalent group. For older children, invite them to count the first set and use that information to replicate it.

For practice, have the children complete the *Picture Match* reproducible on page A23 in the appendix.

Meeting Individual Needs

Make sure children spend enough time working with small numbers before increasing the size of the sets. Note children who always rely on matching to make an equivalent group, without ever using counting. Explicitly model the use of counting by counting the number in one set aloud and then forming another set as you count that number again. Then say, for example, *I have five green ones and five blue ones. The number of green ones is equal to (or the same as) the number of blue ones.*

REFERENCE/FURTHER READING

Ginsburg, Herbert P., and Barbrina Ertle. 2008. "Knowing the Mathematics in Early Childhood Mathematics." In *Contemporary Perspectives on Mathematics in Early Childhood Education*, ed. Olivia N. Saracho and Bernard Spodek, 45–66. New York: Information Age.

Mathematical Focus

- Use tactile information to decide which bag holds fewer or more items.
- Count or match to check predictions.

Potential Challenges and Misconceptions

When items in two sets cannot be counted individually, it is challenging to compare them. Yet making such decisions is a common everyday practice. We might have a sense of how many apples we want to buy, but then choose a bag without actually counting the apples. Children should have opportunities to make such comparisons as well.

The language of comparisons can be problematic. Perhaps you have heard grammatical complaints about the common grocery sign *12 items or less*. The term *fewer* is considered correct when referring to countable objects, for example, *I bought fewer pears than apples*. We use *less* when we refer to amounts that are not countable or for time and money, for example, *Let's use that table because this one has less space* or *The event will last less than two hours*. When we compare 3 and 5, the numerals are not themselves countable, and they could be referring to apples or hours. As a result, the terms *more* and *less* pervade mathematics curriculum materials, and our symbols > and < are referred to as *greater than* and *less than*. We do not need children to make this distinction, but it is reasonable for you to use *fewer* when it is grammatically correct and for them to include the word in their vocabulary.

In the Classroom

Fill two to four different-color opaque bags with same-size counters. Use numbers appropriate to your students. Cloth bags with drawstring openings are ideal. One preschool teacher was able to get a local jeweler to donate bags, while a kindergarten teacher found a parent volunteer to make them. Place a different amount in each bag.

One preschool teacher holds up two bags. (There are four counters in the yellow bag and two in the red one.) She says, "I wonder if you can tell which bag has more just by using your fingers?" Then she passes the bags around for the children to touch, but not open. Some children jiggle the bags, some hold each bag in a different hand as if using a balance scale, and some try to count the number in each bag by feeling the objects. Once everyone has decided, the children open up the bags and match the items. They decide which bag had more and comment on their predictions. The class then considers another example, but this time the children must predict which bag has fewer counters.

A kindergarten teacher uses the bags in a different way. He gives six bags to a small group of children and has them separate the bags into two groups based on whether they think there are fewer than or more than five counters in each bag. Then the children check their predictions.

Consider using the following tasks with the bags:

- Call out a specific number, for example, two, and have the children predict and check to find a bag with that number of counters. For greater challenge, show the numeral rather than say the number name.
- Include two bags with the same number of counters within a group of bags and challenge the children to find them.
- To challenge your most-ready learners, have them place three, or even four, bags in order from least to greatest number of counters and then count to check.

Meeting Individual Needs

The number of items in each bag has a significant effect on the difficulty of these activities. Decreasing the number of objects or increasing the differences among the amounts in the bags makes the activities less challenging and more appropriate for younger children. The shapes of the counters also matter. It is often possible to use touch to determine the number of cubes in a bag, allowing greater success for some children who are sight-impaired. Counters that are small and thin are more difficult to count by touch. Posting an ordered list of the numbers can help some students. Placing the items in clear bags can support students whose visual skills are better than their kinesthetic ones.

REFERENCE/FURTHER READING

Baratta-Lorton, Mary. 1976. *Mathematics Their Way*. Menlo Park, CA: Addison-Wesley.

More, Less, or the Same?

Mathematical Focus
- Compare quantities of objects of unlike sizes.
- Make predictions.

Potential Challenges and Misconceptions
Young children find it challenging to compare the number of objects in two containers, particularly when the objects are not the same size. Very young children might struggle to identify which carton has more balls in it if the containers are the same size and one holds soccer balls and the other holds four-square balls. A student must count the sets by looking at them in the containers or match the sets in his or her mind's eye. It is difficult to ignore the size of the objects and attend to their quantity. If the size of the objects is smaller or the number of them is greater, the challenge increases. Children need many opportunities to make this type of comparison.

In the Classroom
Children really enjoy predicting (guessing) which jar has more objects. The following two activities are engaging and should be played frequently using different materials.

- *Which Jar Has More?*
  Fill two large clear jars with similar objects of different sizes. For example, you might use crayons in one jar and put large markers in the second jar. Or, you might fill one jar with ping-pong balls and the second jar with tennis balls. Begin with fewer than five objects in each jar and increase the number as students become ready for more of a challenge.

  Set the stage the way a magician begins a trick. Present the two jars in which there are a different number of different-size objects. Cover the jars with a piece of cloth. Slowly, ever so slowly, remove the cloth and entice the children to predict which jar has more objects and record the letter of the jar. Before counting the number of objects, ask the students to predict the number of items they think are in jar A and then to make a similar prediction for jar B. Dramatize with flair the act of pouring out the contents and orally counting the number of items in each jar, noticeably touching each item to reinforce one-to-one correspondence. Write A and B on chart paper or the board and record the amounts. Have the children identify the jar that had the greater number of items and compare the outcome with their predictions. Repeat the process, changing the type of objects and inviting volunteers to demonstrate the counts. Continue while student interest is high and repeat often with different counters and quantities.

- *Take a Handful*
  Select two students to take a handful of counters from two large containers. For example, one child might get a handful of teddy bear counters and the other, a handful of color tiles. Before each child releases the items in his or her hands, ask the other children, *Which handful do you think has more counters?* Record the predictions on the board. Then ask the volunteers to open their fists to let the other children see the counters in their hands. Before they count the counters, ask, *Who do you think has fewer counters, Juan or Felicia?* Then each child releases the items one at a time as the class counts and you touch each counter to again reinforce one-to-one correspondence. After the group has counted both handfuls and you have recorded their numbers on the board, ask which child had more and which child had fewer counters.

This early prediction process sets the foundation for thinking about the size of objects relative to a container and the fact that fewer larger objects than smaller objects are needed to fill a container. This inverse relationship is an important concept about measurement. It also introduces making and testing conjectures, which is the informal precursor to understanding proof. Many teachers make a conjecture board on which they record the children's predictions or conjectures. They erase each incorrect prediction or conjecture, leaving visible only those that are mathematically sound.

Meeting Individual Needs
Some children hesitate to make predictions. Rather than make a public declaration, they may find it easier to whisper their predictions to you or a classmate.

The number of objects should match the competency the children have demonstrated with one-to-one correspondence. Encourage children who demonstrate confidence and accuracy in making predictions to compare smaller objects in the containers so when they check their accuracy, the count may go as high as seven or ten.

REFERENCE/FURTHER READING
Diezmann, Carmel. 2008. "On-the-Spot Assessments." *Teaching Children Mathematics* 15 (5): 290–94.

Mathematical Focus

- Make and read graphs.
- Compare data in graphs.

Potential Challenges and Misconceptions

A picture speaks a thousand words, and in mathematics that picture is often a graph. The earlier children interact with graphs, the more likely they are to relate to them as a way of illustrating comparisons. Real and pictorial graphs build skills necessary for later work with bar graphs. They are effective representations that engage young children in making comparisons of more, less, and the same. Using real graphs—graphs formed by children standing in lines under the appropriate headings—provides the concrete experience that prekindergartners need. To avoid misconceptions of graphs, move slowly and carefully toward more abstract representations. For example, begin with children placing themselves on the graph and transition to having them place real objects on the graph, and finally to placing pictures of themselves or the objects on the graph.

In the Classroom

Young children really enjoy active learning. Building graphs should be an interactive activity where the children first model a real graph on the floor before using pictures to represent graphs on a magnetic board or paper hanging on a wall. Create an open space in your room or take the students to the gym or recess area. Over time, pose a variety of questions that have only two possible responses, for example, *With which foot do you kick a ball?* Have children dramatize kicking a ball (or actually kick one). Most children won't recognize whether they use their right or left foot, so have volunteers demonstrate each option with their backs to the children. Then place a left sneaker and a right sneaker about 3 feet from one another. One at a time, have the children demonstrate how they kick and then stand behind the appropriate sneaker. When the children are finished, ask them, *How can we know if more of us kick with our left feet or right feet?* Some children may refer to the perception that one line is much longer, others may suggest counting off, and others may suggest matching the kickers in each line one-to-one. Later in the year or with older students, pose the same question, but instead of having the children stand in lines, have them place their shoes in two rows as representations. Count aloud as a group, touching each of the right shoes, and place a numeral representing the quantity above the right sneaker. Then count the left shoes and place the numeral representing the quantity above the left sneaker. Ask, *Are there more children who kick with their right feet or their left feet?*

Responses to yes-or-no questions can always be graphed. Here are some other possible topics for graphing:

- *Right- or left-handedness:* You might use finger paints to coat each child's dominant hand with paint. The child then presses the hand on a graph outlined on large newsprint or easel paper. If you don't want to use finger paints, the children can pair up to outline each other's hands.
- *Mittens or gloves:* Ask each child to place a mitten on a graph in the Mittens column if he or she wore mittens to school or a glove in the Gloves column if he or she wore gloves.
- *Preferred stories:* Children have preferences about stories they hear and are interested to learn how many of their classmates like the same stories. Choose two books your class has recently explored and ask the children to identify the one they liked best by standing in that column or, if the group is able, by writing their first names.

After children have extensive experience with making graphs that compare two categories, you can expand the graphs to three categories. This is usually done with four- and five-year-olds. Ask a question such as *How did you get to school?* Label each column with a picture of a bus, a car, or a pair of feet. Have children stand in a line behind the picture that best represents their transportation. Ask, *How many arrived by car?* Instruct the children in the car column to count off. Record the number next to a picture of a car that is displayed on an easel. Repeat the process with those that took the bus and those who walked. Ask questions that elicit comparisons among the methods of transportation. If the children are ready, follow up with students making the same graph by placing their pictures on a smaller graph on the bulletin board.

Meeting Individual Needs

More-ready learners can maintain a graph representing the amount of snowy days, rainy days, and sunny days over a month's time. The graph should hang in a prominent area of the classroom. During circle time, after a general discussion about the weather, a volunteer or the leader of the day attaches a picture of a pair of boots, an umbrella, or a sunny face on the graph. At the end of the month, the class counts the number of snowy, rainy, and sunny days.

REFERENCE/FURTHER READING

Clements, Douglas, and Julie Sarama. 2000. "Standards for Preschoolers." *Teaching Children Mathematics* 7 (1): 38–41.

Mathematical Focus
- Model problem situations.
- Use matching or counting to solve comparison problems.

Potential Challenges and Misconceptions

Problem solving should be a central aspect of mathematical explorations. Problems require that children make connections among language, situations, and numbers. Yet too often, young children are not given the opportunity to solve problems.

When possible, offer children story problems that connect to other areas of the curriculum. Lack of such connections can create the idea that mathematics does not relate to the other subjects. Be sure to review vocabulary associated with story problems before exploring the problems. Many learners can be distracted by words they don't know, even if knowing their meanings isn't necessary to find solutions to the problems.

Children who know that seven comes after six in the counting sequence do not necessarily recognize that a group of seven items is greater than a group of six items, as they may not have connected these two aspects of counting yet. Some learners may do so and be able to immediately identify which number is more or less. Have them explain their thinking so that others are exposed to this reasoning.

In the Classroom

A dramatic play center can offer many props for story problems. One teacher has collected a variety of hats. She has two students dramatize the following situation as she describes it.

> Mr. Green has a fire hat, a ski cap, and a top hat.
> [The teacher directs a boy to gather the hats and place them in front of him.]
> Mrs. Green has a baseball cap and a sun hat.
> [The teacher has a girl gather these hats and place them in front of her.]

Then the teacher asks, "Who has fewer hats, Mr. Green or Mrs. Green?" When the children agree that it is Mrs. Green, she asks, "What could you do to show me that this is true?"

Children's literature can also provide contexts for story problems. A kindergarten class is focusing on the author Eric Carle. After reading *The Very Hungry Caterpillar* (1987), the children pretend to be other caterpillars that are very hungry. The teacher tells stories similar to the following one as the children use felt pieces or counters to model the situation.

> There was one caterpillar that was very, very hungry.
> One day he ate seven apples.
> Another day he ate six pears.
> Did the caterpillar eat more apples or pears?

Classroom manipulatives can also suggest story problems. The *Bear Land* reproducible on page A24 in the appendix shows a picture of a cave and a tree. You can create a variety of problems that tell the number of bears near the cave and the number of bears near the tree. The students can use teddy bear counters to represent the bears. Then they can compare the groups. Be sure you include an example with the same number of bears in each location. Asking about more or less in connection with sets that have the same quantity can emphasize the meaning of equal. You can decide whether the children should record their findings, perhaps circling the number that is more or less.

Meeting Individual Needs

Stories that identify three objects in a set, one at a time, are easier for young learners to model than stories that say, for example, that there are three hats. However, such stories usually contain more words, and the amount of language may overwhelm some learners. For English language learners, be sure to include actual objects (realia) and gestures whenever possible.

When we make connections between literature and mathematics, we help some students better understand the contexts of the problems. If you choose a favorite book, you may also provide motivation for the activity.

For those learners ready for a greater challenge, read a poem such as "Band-Aids," by Shel Silverstein (1974, 140), and have the children pose their own comparison problems about bandages.

REFERENCES/FURTHER READING

Carle, Eric. 1987. *The Very Hungry Caterpillar.* New York: Philomel Books.

Greenes, Carole E., Linda Dacey, Mary Cavanagh, Carol R. Findell, Linda J. Sheffield, and Marian Small. 2004. *Navigating Through Problem Solving and Reasoning in Prekindergarten–Kindergarten.* Reston, VA: National Council of Teachers of Mathematics.

Silverstein, Shel. 1974. *Where the Sidewalk Ends: The Poems and Drawings of Shel Silverstein.* New York: HarperCollins.

Mathematical Focus

- Use the symbols = and ≠.
- Create equal and unequal sets.

Potential Challenges and Misconceptions

In general, teachers give more attention to the term *equal* than to *not equal*, yet children in kindergarten are expected to be familiar with the symbols for both. Young students will find it easier to meet this requirement if the phrases are introduced in prekindergarten. It is also important that children understand the idea that if a number is more or less than another number, it is not equal to that number. Some children find it challenging to make the necessary connections among these ideas. Being attentive to when children identify something as being unfair, due to unequal numbers, can help ensure that learners connect these concepts.

In the Classroom

Most young learners enjoy linking cubes to make trains or building towers with blocks. They often make comparative statements based on ideas of measurement. It is common to hear children use the words *taller*, *higher*, *longer*, and *bigger* when they compare what they have built. Children should also compare these structures by number. Following are some activities that encourage such comparisons.

- Say "Go!" and have two children link cubes in a row for five to ten seconds (depending on how quickly the children build and how high they can count) and then compare their trains. Two- and three-year-olds are likely to compare the lengths, without necessarily starting them at a common endpoint. This is developmentally appropriate and involves the children in the comparative process. Encourage them to then count the number of cubes in each train and to make a comparative statement about their trains. Then you can ask about whether the numbers of cubes in the trains are equal or not equal.
- Repeat the previous activity with cubes that can be linked on multiple sides and have the children make buildings. This arrangement will make initial visual comparisons more challenging. Then have the children undo the links and count to compare.
- Follow a similar process but have the children make towers with blocks. Again, children may attend to a measure (height) rather than the number of blocks. Examples with blocks of different sizes can be most challenging, as a tower could be taller but have fewer blocks. Such an example emphasizes the importance of not relying exclusively on visual images to decide which has more.
- You can introduce the symbols = and ≠ at the kindergarten level. Talk about what the symbols mean. Write the number sentence 5 ≠ 6 and ask the children to read it. Have volunteers suggest other sentences you could write using the same symbol. Then repeat the process, writing 6 = 6. Finally, write the numbers 7 and 9 and ask which sign should be used to show their relationship.
- Children in kindergarten can use same-size cubes or blocks to play *Make It*. Make copies of the *Relationship Cards* reproducible on page A25 in the appendix and cut out and laminate the cards. Review the meanings of the words and symbols with the children and model the activity with a volunteer player. Shuffle the cards and place them facedown in a pile. The first player creates a tower out of the cubes or blocks. The second player turns over the top card and makes a tower to match the relationship shown on the card (more, less, =, ≠). Then the players switch roles. As the children play, observe them to see how the second player decides what number of cubes or blocks to use. Does the child build a matching tower visually and then adjust it if the goal is to make it not equal to the first tower? Does the child count the number of blocks used in each tower? Does the child make a tower that uses one or two more or less blocks or make a tower of a very different amount?

Meeting Individual Needs

The universal sign for *no* is a circle with a backslash. Students may have seen a No Parking or No Turning sign that uses such a format. Unfortunately, the "not equal" sign uses a forward slash, but familiarity with such signs does help children recognize a slash as meaning *no*. Making this connection may help some students remember what the sign means.

It is easier for children to recognize these symbols than to write them. Be sure to have images of both signs available when students are expected to write them.

Some of your students may be able to compare more than two numbers and numbers up to twenty. Others may be able to do so only with two numbers up to three or five. Some children can compare numerals using a mental number line, while others must count or match real objects or counters. The *Comparison Assessment Form* reproducible (see page A26 in the appendix) can help you note these differences as you observe them and thus support your ability to meet individual differences.

REFERENCE/FURTHER READING

Sprung, Barbara. 2006. "Yes You Can! Meeting the Challenge of Math and Science." *Early Childhood Today* 3 (20): 44–52.

At the Playground

A27

Mathematical Focus
- Dramatize addition story problems.
- Interpret the language of addition.

Potential Challenges and Misconceptions

Think about all the events that occur throughout a child's day that can be mathematized, that is, seen through the lens of mathematics. These daily occurrences lend themselves to addition story problems. Learners at this level can consider two types of addition situations. The first is a *change-plus* problem. For example:

> There are three children at the learning center. Two more children join them. How many children are at the learning center now?

In this type of problem, an initial set is given, another set joins it, and the children must determine the new total.

> The second type is a *put-together* problem. For example:

> There are three children painting at the art center. There are two children using clay at the art center. How many children are at the art center?

In this type of problem, two groups exist already, and students must put them together and find the total number. No actual change occurs.

Some learners may find one type of problem more challenging than the other, so it is important to pose both types for students to solve. You should not teach the children these distinctions.

Initially, children should dramatize addition situations using real objects. Two- and three-year-olds may work solely with objects while four- and five-year-olds will progress to using pictures of real objects, counters, fingers, or drawings to represent addition story problems. When appropriate, you can introduce the use of a number sentence to four- and five-year-olds. The number sentences can be built using prepared number and operator cards that the children put together to represent the story.

In the Classroom

On the playground, a preschool teacher is comforting Melissa, who accidentally tripped Jodi. The fall caused a scraped knee. Then Melissa looks over at the swings and exclaims, "Look, Jodi is headed for the swings. Her knee must be better!"

Before returning inside, the teacher gathers the children around the swings and says, "Melissa and I were looking at the swings. Sophia and Chloe were on the swings and Jodi joined them. How many children were on the swings then?" There are a number of responses, including "Three," "Two," and "Jodi." "Let's act it out," the teacher suggests. Sophia and Chloe get on the swings and the teacher points to each as she says, "One, two. There are two children on the swings." Then she asks Jodi to join them. The children say the numbers one to three as the teacher points to each child. The teacher then summarizes,

"There were two children on the swings. One more child came to swing. Now there are three children on the swings."

They explore the same basic problem a couple of more times, using the names of different children and, thus, new actors. On another day, they dramatize situations involving the slide and the sandbox. Later the teacher works with a couple of children and a copy of the *Playground Stories* reproducible on page A27 in the appendix. She tells them an addition story problem about one child sliding down the slide and three children climbing up the slide ladder. She helps the children use plastic people manipulatives to model the problem on the mat. Then she asks the children to retell the story in their own words.

A kindergarten teacher gathers her students in the rug area and shows them a problem written on chart paper. She points to each word as she reads:

> There are four children on the swings. There are two children on the slide. How many children is that together?

She rereads the problem a couple of times, with the children joining her by memory. She asks a couple of children to restate the problem in their own words and then asks how they could act it out. As Jayden points to two different areas of the rug, he suggests, "We could pretend that's the swings and over there is the slide." The teacher chooses volunteers who dramatize the situation. Then the teacher says, "We have four and two more and that is the same as, or equal to, six," as she writes $4 + 2 = 6$.

Then the teacher asks the children to turn to a partner and gives each of the pairs a copy of the *Playground Stories* reproducible and some plastic people. She poses two more problems that the children model on the mats, and each time she has the children restate the problem and talk with their partners about how to model it. Once all agree on the answer, she writes the related number sentence on the chart paper.

Meeting Individual Needs

It is important that children work with real objects as long as needed. Some young learners can use pictures of such objects or felt pieces made to resemble them. Some children are comfortable with more abstract counters if the counters share an important attribute with the real objects. For example, red and green tiles might be used to represent a story about buying red apples and green apples. Over time, more abstract representations, such as circles or tally marks, can be introduced and adopted.

REFERENCE/FURTHER READING

McGee, Mileen. 2005. "Hidden Mathematics in the Preschool Classroom." *Teaching Children Mathematics* 11 (6): 345–47.

A7, A28

Mathematical Focus

- Model subtraction problems.
- Interpret the language of subtraction.

Potential Challenges and Misconceptions

As with addition, subtraction situations are common, everyday experiences. Pencils are taken from the pencil can and red crayons are separated from blue ones. You can model two types of subtraction story problems with learners at this stage. The first is a *change-minus* problem. For example:

> Janelle has four carrot sticks at snack time. She eats three of them. How many carrot sticks does Janelle have left?

Note that there is a given set and a change takes place; that is, some items are no longer in the group. The task is to find the number of items that remain.

The second type is a *take-apart* problem. For example:

> Diego is playing with five toy cars. Three of the cars are green. The other cars are red. How many cars are red?

The total number of the original set is given in this type of problem as well. Then a subset of the group is identified, though it doesn't leave the group. In this case, the goal is to identify the number of other items in the set.

Though these are considered different types of problems, children are likely to model both by separating the whole set into two parts, and that is fine. As with addition, we're sharing the distinctions between these problem types with you to help you vary the problems you pose; you should not teach them to your children. The goal for children is to become familiar with the language of these problems and to model the different situations related to subtraction. Without such exposure, children often develop the misconception that subtraction is only used when a problem asks about how many are left.

In the Classroom

Tie both ends of a long piece of blue ribbon (big enough to identify a large portion of the rug area) together and use it to designate an imaginary pond. Gather the children around the "pond." Given story problems about a pond, all children can model the stories themselves, and older children can hold puppets or people manipulatives that they can use to dramatize the situations. Invite the children to share some of their own experiences related to swimming. Then introduce problems that build on these experiences. For example, when Justin talked about having to leave the water once because his teeth were chattering, his teacher posed the following problem:

> There are four children swimming in the pond. Justin is so cold that he needs to get out of the water. How many children are swimming now?

The teacher stated, "Let's see what that looks like," and asked

You could also begin by asking volunteers to dramatize water activities. In one classroom, children act out a variety of activities: swimming, jumping, diving, and playing Marco Polo. Over time, be sure to include both types of subtraction problems, for example:

Change-Minus	Take-Apart
There are five children on the dock. Three of the children jump into the water. How many children are left on the dock?	There are six children in the water. Two of the children are swimming. The other children are playing Marco Polo. How many children are playing Marco Polo?

For small-group work, make copies of the *Pond Stories* reproducible on page A28 in the appendix, which shows a picture of a pond scene. An adult should work directly with younger pre-K learners to model the same problems with manipulatives and these pictures. People or frog manipulatives could be used, along with new related stories, for older pre-K children. Eventually, kindergarten children can work with partners or independently. They can make drawings or even equations to represent their thinking. Be sure to explicitly connect a subtraction situation to a number sentence; for example, $6 - 2 = 4$ represents the Marco Polo problem suggested. Read this as *six minus (or subtract) two is equal to four*.

Meeting Individual Needs

It is essential that the story problems include numbers of appropriate size as well as contexts that are familiar to your students. Feel free to change the pond scenarios to that of a pool, if a pool is more familiar to the children. Listen closely to the informal conversations of ELL students. Perhaps you can embrace their cultures by creating problems about an upcoming celebration or special food they have mentioned.

If it has been a while since you have assessed your students' abilities to count, you may want to do so. (Use the *Counting Assessment Form* reproducible on page A7 in the appendix.)

Children can become confused when they adopt more abstract techniques for representing subtraction situations. For example, after separating the whole into two groups, they may not be certain which group they should count. Some children find it helpful to verbalize the story as they model it. Others may benefit from making drawings or using manipulatives more directly related to the problem.

REFERENCE/FURTHER READING

Lo Cicero, Ana M., Karen C. Fuson, and Martha Allexsaht-Snider. 1999. "Mathematizing Children's Stories, Helping Children Solve Word Problems, and Supporting Parental Involvement." In *Changing the Faces of Mathematics: Perspectives on Latinos*, ed. Luis Ortiz-Franco, Norma G. Hernandez, and Yolanda De La Cruz, 59–70. Reston, VA: National Council of Teachers of Mathematics.

Mathematical Focus

- Model addition and subtraction.
- Use cookie sheets and box tops to organize counting.

Potential Challenges and Misconceptions

Counting skills are necessary for success with addition and subtraction. Young children add by counting on, and some have trouble keeping track of which items they have counted. Others may need support when separating sets into two groups. Many young learners lack the fine-motor skills necessary to work with small counters. With appropriate scaffolding, these children can be successful at modeling addition and subtraction.

In the Classroom

Most young learners engage easily with pattern blocks. Children are attracted to bright colors and are interested in designs they can form when placing blocks together. Andrews (2004) suggests putting magnetic tape on the backs of the blocks and using them on inexpensive metal cookie sheets. The use of these materials keeps the blocks in place and greatly benefits young learners with emerging fine-motor skills. Andrews suggests using the blocks this way for geometric explorations, but they can support number sense as well.

A preschool teacher has the children use the magnetized blocks and cookie sheets to model story problems. She refers to the blocks by their colors and shapes. This helps the children identify the blocks while being exposed to their appropriate names. She begins by holding up a green triangle and asks the children the color and name of the shape. She then repeats the process with the orange square. Depending on the readiness of the children, she may use only these two shapes, or she may also introduce the trapezoid, rhombus, and hexagon pieces and have the children repeat each word three times. Next she has them gather sets of blocks with questions such as *Who can show me two green triangles?* Then she might pose the following addition problems, which she instructs the children to model:

Brady has five blue rhombuses. He gets two more blue rhombuses. How many rhombuses does he have altogether?	Heather makes a design with the blocks. She uses three green triangles. She uses four orange squares. How many blocks does she use in her design?

She also poses subtraction problems, such as the following:

Shana has eight green triangles. Then she gives five of them to Alice. How many triangles does Shana have now?	Luke has six blocks. He has three yellow hexagons. The other blocks are red trapezoids. How many of Luke's blocks are red trapezoids?

Since the children are modeling the problems, they can count the blocks to arrive at the appropriate sum or difference.

You can also combine geometric thinking and addition by giving four- and five-year-olds a specific space to fill and identifying two sets of blocks they should use. The children use the blocks to fill the space and record or tell an adult the total number of blocks involved. Examples are provided in the *Pattern Block Fill-In* reproducible on page A29 in the appendix. Students can place the figures on the cookie sheets and arrange the blocks on top of them. Younger children can do this with an adult's guidance.

Box tops can also be used to support students' modeling. Turn a top over, cut a notch into the center of the lip on each of the long sides, and place a bright ribbon through the notches. When modeling addition problems, instruct the children to place a specified number of counters on each side of the ribbon to represent each addend. Students can then remove the counters from the box top as they count the items to find their total. For subtraction problems, children can place the total on the left side of the top and then move the number taken away or set apart to the right side. Then they can count the objects that remain on the left side. The figure shows how to model $5 - 2 = 3$.

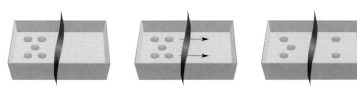

Meeting Individual Needs

Kindergarten children who are able to do so can record a number sentence for each of the three pattern block examples on the *Pattern Block Fill-In* reproducible. For greater challenge, you can create areas to be filled and identify the types of blocks that students should use, but not their numbers. The children can then record the number of each shape they used as well as the number of total blocks.

Many children will be challenged by the different names of the shapes, but even two- and three-year-olds can use them with a lot of repetition, so avoid referring to the blocks by only their colors. Over time, drop inclusion of the color when naming the shapes.

REFERENCE/FURTHER READING

Andrews, Angela G. 2004. "Adapting Manipulatives to Foster the Thinking of Young Children." *Teaching Children Mathematics* 11 (1): 15–17.

Mathematical Focus

- Count or subitize to find the number of items that remains.
- Count all or count on to find the total number.

Potential Challenges and Misconceptions

Subitizing is the ability to recognize the quantity in a group without counting the individual items. Some children can use this skill when they model an addition or subtraction situation. They might use their fingers to model a story involving $5 + 3$. Showing five fingers at once, rather than counting to five, is an efficient way to represent the first addend. To model $6 - 4$, a student can show six fingers and then fold down four of them. Many children will subitize rather than count the two fingers that remain.

To find $5 + 2$, whether given in a story problem, in a question such as *What is two more than five?* or as an expression to complete ($5 + 2 = $ ____), most young children first represent each group and then count all of the items, beginning at one. An important developmental benchmark occurs, usually in kindergarten or grade one, when children count on to find the total. Using fingers as well as common arrangements of sets encourage students to subitize. Confidence with such configurations is often a precursor to counting on, rather than counting all, to find the total number.

Some teachers express concern that children will become overly dependent on their fingers and don't allow their use. Many mathematics educators disagree with this attitude and have for some time. In 1979, Zaslavsky suggested that teachers encourage children to use their fingers to help them count and pointed out that number words in a variety of languages originated from names for gestures. More recent research supports this encouragement for young children to use fingers to develop their counting skills (Jordan et al. 2008).

Some children have been taught to use their fingers in a specific way or believe there is only one right way to use them. As younger children tend to explore numbers only to five, they may work in a prescribed manner, that is, showing one addend on each hand. Though this technique allows for a clear representation of each addend, it becomes problematic when numbers greater than five are included. Unless intervention is deemed necessary, it is better to let the children make their own decisions as to how they will use their fingers.

In the Classroom

One teacher puts magnetic tape on the backs of counters. In preparation for her meeting with a small group of learners, she places three of the counters in a row on a metal cookie tray and covers the tray with a piece of construction paper. She also has some extra magnetized counters. She tells the children that there are counters on the tray and that she will show them the tray quickly and then cover it again. She explains, "Your job is to figure out how many counters are on the tray." She uncovers the tray for a moment and covers it again. The students tell how many counters they saw, and then she uncovers the tray again so they can verify their answers. After they all agree there are three counters, she asks the children to show her that many fingers. She observes who counts by ones and

Next the teacher replaces the paper cover and puts one more counter below the three already there (see figure). She follows the same procedure as before and then asks, "How did you know that there were four?"

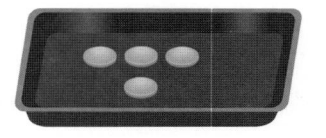

Brian offers, "We knew three." He holds up three fingers. "So one more is four." Then Brian puts up one more finger and shows everyone his four fingers. The group considers some other examples, and the teacher leaves the counters, tray, and paper cover out during choice time. The following week the teacher introduces a similar activity with the same materials, but this time she takes counters off the tray and children lower their fingers to represent the action.

The *Visualize It* reproducible on page A30 in the appendix has four cards containing pictures of familiar objects. Make a copy of it and cut the cards apart. Show each card quickly to a small group of children and then ask them to tell how many items they saw. Encourage the children to give details as they describe how they decided on the total number. After a couple of children have shared their thinking, summarize, for example, *So you saw three right away and then one more, and that is the same as four.* Ask kindergarten children, *What number sentence can we write to show what we saw?* Discuss both $3 + 1 = 4$ and $4 = 3 + 1$. Note that it is fine if the 3 and 1 are in reverse order.

Meeting Individual Needs

Children who are still developing grade-level language have access to problems presented visually. These children often enjoy activities involving quick images because the learners recognize that they have a greater opportunity for success.

Some children do not have significant exposure to dice, dominoes, or playing cards; thus, they are less familiar with the common arrangements used to represent numbers. Make sure such materials are available during choice time or included in a mathematics learning center.

As you work with greater numbers, ask children to first draw what they think they saw. Then show the visual model again for them to check their predictions. Some learners attend more closely to details once they have something in front of them to check. Over time, some children are able to describe the details they tend to miss, as Willow demonstrated when she said, "I always get the big group, but I miss some of the spread-out ones."

REFERENCES/FURTHER READING

Jordan, Nancy C., David Kaplan, Chaitanya Ramineni, and Maria N. Locuniak. 2008. "Development of Number Combination Skill in the Early School Years: When Do *Fingers* Help?" *Developmental Science* 11 (5): 662–68.

Weiland, Linnea. 2007. "Experiences to Help Children Learn to Count On." *Teaching Children Mathematics* 14 (3): 188–91.

Zaslavsky, Claudia. 1979. "It's OK to Count on Your Fingers." *Teacher* 96 (6) 54–56.

Mathematical Focus

- Decompose numbers.
- Record ways a number can be separated into two groups.

Potential Challenges and Misconceptions

Eventually, children are expected to add and subtract small numbers by visualizing them, rather than modeling them. This ability helps learners move to fluency with basic facts at the later grades.

Some children experience conversations such as the following as part of their normal daily interactions:

Child: I want more crackers.
Parent: How many crackers do you have now?
Child: Two.
Parent: You can have one more. How many crackers will you have then?

Other children are not exposed to such thinking and need many opportunities to compose and decompose (put together and break apart) numbers. NCTM suggests that children be given opportunities to find the "partners hiding inside small numbers" (Fuson, Clements, and Beckmann 2010, 40). For example, children could separate a group of four objects to find that the partners 1 and 3, 2 and 2, and 3 and 1 are hidden in 4. Such activities support the visualization of numbers and help learners transition to being able to answer questions such as *What is one more than three?*

There are many misconceptions about the equal sign. In fact, many children and adults interpret it as a mere indicator of where the answer should be written. Partner problems start with the whole, which is then taken apart or decomposed. When starting with four objects and finding they can be separated into three and one, a recording such as $4 = 3 + 1$ makes good sense to children using equations. When learners see equations written in different formats, they are more likely to understand the equal sign as meaning *is the same as*.

In the Classroom

One teacher spray paints metal washers red on one side and blue on the other side. She has worked with children of multiple ages and found that she can use these materials with a wide variety of learners. Depending on the age or readiness of the learners, she changes the number of washers she uses and adapts her expectation for how the children should respond to them. She always begins by having the children place two to ten of the washers in a pencil can. Then they shake the can and empty out the washers onto a rug sample, noting what they see. With two- and three-year-olds, she begins with two or three washers. With three washers that all land showing red, the children count them. If the children see two red washers and one blue, they count each color as well as the total number. The teacher says, *Yes, when we have two red and one blue, we have three washers in all.*

When working with four-year-olds, the teacher has the children put up to five washers in the can and has them use blue and red crayons to record the different outcomes. They work in pairs, with an adult nearby, and there are many conversations about whether they have found a new way to make five. Eventually, equations are introduced but not required.

Five to ten washers can be put in the can when working with kindergartners, and both drawings and numbers may be included in their recordings. Some children may record the number of each color, while others will write equations. When all the washers show the same color, most children will just put them back in the can and shake again. A few children will include zero in their work.

Children in kindergarten can also be asked to solve story problems that suggest the need to identify all of the number partners but do not state the task explicitly. For example, one classroom is studying the seasons and taking a city walk to look for signs of spring. During their walk, they stop to look at tulips planted in front of an apartment building. They talk about how bright the colors are and how the yellow ones remind them of the sun.

The next day the teacher poses the following problem:

> Melissa picked six tulips. Some of the tulips are red. The other tulips are yellow. How many tulips of each color did Melissa pick?

After the teacher reads the problem twice, the children restate it and talk about strategies they can use to solve it. The teacher gives each student a recording sheet with the problem written at the top and sets them off to work independently, in pairs, or in a small group with the teacher. Later, they will come back together to share their findings.

Meeting Individual Needs

Schulman and Eston (1998) suggest that kindergarten teachers can present problems such as the flower one several times throughout the kindergarten year, changing the context as class activities evolve. Initially, most students will guess and check with objects until they find one combination that yields the correct total. Over the course of the year, many of the children will find multiple solutions, and their recording strategies will become more sophisticated. Some children will be able to identify all of the possibilities for totals up to ten. Open-ended problems such as this one let all of the children participate at some level and thus strengthen the classroom learning community while meeting individual needs. Revisiting this type of problem provides important assessment data, allowing you to document learning over time.

REFERENCES/FURTHER READING

Fuson, Karen C., Douglas H. Clements, and Sybilla Beckmann. 2010. *Focus in Prekindergarten: Teaching with Curriculum Focal Points.* Reston, VA: National Council of Teachers of Mathematics.

Schulman, Linda, and Rebeka Eston. 1998. "A Problem Worth Revisiting." *Teaching Children Mathematics* 5 (2): 72–77.

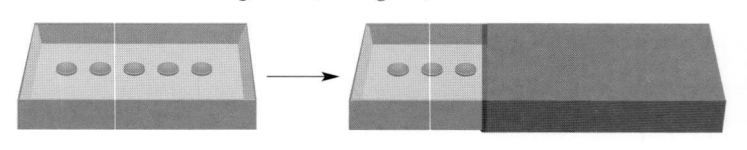

Mathematical Focus

- Visualize sets to determine the number of hidden objects.
- Count to identify missing addends.

Potential Challenges and Misconceptions

Most people find it easier to count forward than count backward, to add rather than subtract. So it is mathematically powerful to make connections between these two actions, to realize, for instance, that we can find 7 − 2 by thinking, *What plus two is seven?* It is important for young children to relate the actions of joining and separating, of putting together and taking apart. Learners at the prekindergarten and kindergarten levels can make early associations among these actions, which help build conceptual links between addition and subtraction. Such connections support computational fluency and greater success in later grades.

In the Classroom

Storytelling or dramatic flair can capture children's interest and provide important hooks for learning. There are a variety ways to introduce missing partners. One teacher shows a small group of children four shiny new pennies. The children look at them and count them together. She then talks about how she feels clumsy today and pretends to accidentally knock three of the pennies off the table. "Oh dear," she says. "How many pennies are missing?" The children immediately look under the table to find the pennies and bring them back to the table. She asks, "How do we know we found them all?" The children retell what happened with the pennies and she summarizes, "So we had four pennies and then we had only one penny. We found the three missing pennies, and we are back to four pennies." Just as she finishes, she "accidentally" knocks two of the pennies off the table and repeats the activity.

Children can engage in a variety of follow-up activities to this or similar introductions. For example:

- Give initial experiences where the missing objects are in view. For example, laminate five gray pieces of construction paper and place them across a corner of the rug area, from one side to another. Ask the children to imagine that the rug is a river and that they are going to cross it by walking on the "stones" carefully, one step at a time. Have a few students dramatize walking on the stones, counting each one as they do so. Then have a student stop at the third stone, and ask him or her, *How many more stones are there before you cross to the other side?*
- Working with a small group of children, place three to six teddy bear counters in a row and have the children count them. Next place a crayon somewhere along the row to separate the bears into two groups (see figure). Have the children tell the number in each group and the total.

After doing this several times with the same total, change the activity. This time have the children close their eyes while you remove some of the bears. Ask them to predict the number of bears you are hiding.

- Have a child put two to ten counters in a cup, depending on his or her readiness level. Shake the cup and empty a few of the counters onto the table. Have the child predict how many counters are still in the cup and then count them to check.
- Duplicate the *What's Missing?* reproducible on page A31 in the appendix and have students draw circles to make the set of circles in each row match the quantity indicated by the numeral.
- For interest, include use of a musical instrument such as a triangle or toy xylophone. Name a total number, for example, six. Play four notes on the instrument and ask, *How many more notes should I play?* If the children are ready, have one of them lead the activity.
- Make a strip of dots for a given total, along with a sleeve for the strip. Then you can slide the strip of dots in and out of the sleeve in order to have students predict and then verify the number of missing dots (see figure).

- For children who are ready for more abstract challenges, ask questions such as *I have three. How many more do I need to make five?*

Meeting Individual Needs

These activities can be experienced at a variety of levels. Some children will make predictions that aren't accurate, but they can count to find the correct amount. Allow these learners to stay with a particular total, if some of their predictions are correct. Otherwise, reduce the total number of items. If children are arriving at correct answers quickly, increase the total number in the group, but occasionally return to a lower number to maintain those number partners as well.

Making the given addend or number partner greater than the missing one makes it easier for most learners. For example, given a total of six, it is easier to identify the partner for five than to identify the partner for one.

REFERENCES/FURTHER READING

Copley, Juanita V. 1999. *Mathematics in the Early Years.* Reston, VA: National Council of Teachers of Mathematics.

Fuson, Karen C., Douglas H. Clements, and Sybilla Beckmann. 2010. *Focus in Kindergarten: Teaching with Curriculum Focal Points.* Reston, VA: National Council of Teachers of Mathematics.

Draw It

Mathematical Focus
- Use drawings to model addition and subtraction situations.

Potential Challenges and Misconceptions

Drawings can provide an important transition between using manipulatives and working only with abstract number names. Occasionally, you may want a child to make a drawing to show his or her thinking or to pose a problem. Children often enjoy the process of making elaborate drawings to illustrate their thinking, and such work helps children better understand mathematical ideas (Perry and Dockett 2002). Drawings or recordings can also be shared with others, giving other children access to different ways of thinking.

Such drawings take considerable time, however, and such time is not always available. Some children may discover efficient drawing techniques on their own, but others require explicit modeling of such a technique. The goal is not to teach drawing techniques, which can be learned by rote, but rather to provide access to new ways of thinking.

In the Classroom

One teacher shows the children two trees drawn on the whiteboard. Then she tells the following story problem:

> There are two squirrels under one tree. There are three more squirrels under the other tree. How many squirrels are there altogether?

She repeats the story. After she says, "There are two squirrels under one tree," she makes two marks under the tree while saying, "One, two." She does the same for the three squirrels under the other tree. Then the children talk about and demonstrate how to find the number of all of the squirrels. She tells other stories about birds, bunnies, and children at the two trees, and volunteers at each tree make marks to show the data. Some children make circles, some make lines, and to represent the children, one child makes stick figures but does so quickly.

In another class, the teacher poses the following problem:

> There were four eggs in my refrigerator this morning. Then I had one at breakfast. How many eggs do I have left?

As she tells about the four eggs, she draws four ovals in a row and then counts them. "What happened to the eggs?" she asks.

Argo replies, "You ate one."

Benson giggles while exclaiming, "It's gone!"

The teacher crosses off one of the "eggs" and queries, "So how many eggs are there now?"

The children agree there are three eggs, and then the teacher tells another story problem. This time one child makes the initial set, and another marks off the items to show the change that has taken place.

A kindergarten teacher tells the following story:

> When I was walking to work today, I saw six animals. Four of them were dogs and the rest were cats. How many cats did I see?

Then she retells the problem. When she shares the fact that she saw six animals, she draws six circles in a row, while counting from one to six. After mentioning the four cats, she counts to four aloud while touching the first four circles in the row. Then she draws a line segment to the right of the fourth circle, separating those circles from the others. She asks, "How many cats did I see?" The children discuss the drawing and what it shows, and then the teacher shares other stories while volunteers make the corresponding drawings.

The *Story Drawings* reproducible on page A32 in the appendix has three pictures that can be used for story problems and drawings. You can easily adapt stories to focus only on addition or subtraction. Possible examples are provided on page A33 of the appendix; you can change the numbers as appropriate. Read each problem to a small group of children, and then repeat it slowly as necessary. Have the students make drawings on their copies of the reproducible and tell or record the number that answers the question. You should record the associated number sentence if appropriate. (Note that answers are provided for your reference.)

Meeting Individual Needs

Some children may not yet be comfortable using only circles, lines, dividers, or cross-outs to represent objects, and this is fine. Others may make drawings corresponding to each number, rather than ones that actually model the process suggested. For example, consider this problem:

> There are seven horses by the fence. Then three of the horses walk away. How many horses are still at the fence?

Some children might draw seven circles, three circles, and four circles. While this identifies the two relevant partner numbers for seven, a drawing of seven circles with three of them crossed off would more accurately model the specific situation. Encourage such learners to retell the story as they draw. Some children will change their drawings to more closely replicate the actions in the problem. Either way is fine as long as they recognize the answer and can associate the drawing with the situation.

Children should not be required to make drawings if they are thinking on an abstract level. Allow some learners to record, for instance, a *3* on the elephant to represent the clowns sitting there, rather than circles or tally marks. Other children should be allowed to continue using manipulatives to model problems if they prefer to do so.

REFERENCES/FURTHER READING

Andrews, Angela G., and Paul R. Trafton. 2002. *Little Kids—Powerful Problem Solvers: Math Stories from a Kindergarten Classroom.* Portsmouth, NH: Heinemann.

Lambdin, Diana. 2003. "Benefits of Teaching Through Problem Solving." In *Teaching Mathematics Through Problem Solving: Prekindergarten–Grade 6,* ed. Frank K. Lester, 3–13. Reston, VA: National Council of Teachers of Mathematics.

Perry, Bob, and Sue Dockett. 2002. "Young Children's Access to Powerful Mathematical Ideas." In *Handbook of International Research in Mathematics Education,* ed. Lyn D. English, 81–113. Mahwah, NJ: Erlbaum.

Mathematical Focus

- Pose story problems.
- Use the language of addition and subtraction.

Potential Challenges and Misconceptions

In most classes, it is only the teachers who pose mathematical story problems. To be better prepared for the challenge of applying their mathematical skills to the real world, children need opportunities to pose problems, too, not just to solve them. Children begin school with natural curiosity, and too often, they learn that only the adults decide what will be discussed or investigated. By encouraging problem posing, you can support their initial curiosity and build further on children's interests and ideas.

Posing problems also strengthens students' understanding of mathematics and their familiarity with the language of mathematics. Unfortunately, many of the problems children are asked to solve end in one of two phrases: *How many in all (or altogether)?* or *How many are left?* The formulaic language of some curriculum materials can create the misconception that words associated with addition and subtraction are quite limited. Thinking in their natural language helps children broaden their understanding of addition and subtraction and more easily recognize how to model problems. They can begin to include words such as *then*, *now*, and *next*. These words suggest the sequence of the events and help support children's understanding of how to represent situations.

In the Classroom

Teachers should ask mathematical questions throughout the day. Questions such as *Do you think we have enough paintbrushes? Do I need two or three more folders for this table?* and *How many firefighter hats do we have if we put these boxes of hats together?* suggest that thinking about numbers is common, as is posing questions related to them. Listen to conversations in the art or drama area or at snack time to learn what questions the children are asking about numbers and gather important assessment data. As you listen, note whether a student

- asks questions having to do with the number of objects present or that are needed,
- uses number-related vocabulary (*all*, *some*, *lots*, *more*, *less*), or
- counts to answer questions related to quantities that arise during the day.

When introducing a more focused problem-posing activity, rather than just supporting those that arise, it is best to provide a context that students can consider. Often, children's experiences outside of the home suggest ideas. Questions such as *Have you ever been to a circus (birthday party, or picnic)?* can stimulate conversations about what the children saw and did there. In one classroom, the children talk about how funny they thought it was to see so many clowns come out of a car at the circus. The teacher asks them to make up a number story about clowns and cars.

Children's literature can also foster problem posing. One teacher reads *How Many Fish?* (Cohen 2000) to a group of four- and five-year-olds. There are six fish in the story and one gets lost in one of the children's pails before it is found and released. The students enjoy the simple repetition, rhythm, and rhyme of the fish. A couple of volunteers retell the part of the story about the one missing fish and then she asks the children to pair up to create new problems. A couple of partners pose their problems about different numbers of lost fish, and the children dramatize and answer them.

You can also use pictures to inspire the creation of story problems. One kindergarten teacher showed the following picture, and the children posed these questions:

- Is one cake chocolate?
- How many candles are there?
- How many people get to eat the cakes?
- How many more candles does this cake have?
- What if all the candles don't get blown out?
- How many candles will these cakes have next year?

The children were readily engaged in the activity, interspersing their brainstorming with details about the kind of birthday cakes they liked best or other birthday-related information. The teacher was not surprised that nearly all of the questions were about the candles, since that was the feature of the cakes that differed. She tries to use pictures that draw the students' attention to combining or comparing numbers of items.

The *Picnic Story Problems* reproducible on page A34 in the appendix shows a picnic table and some animals. Make copies to share with a small group of children. Younger children can just ask questions such as *How many squirrels are there?* Encourage more-ready or older learners to create stories about groups that are joined or separated.

Meeting Individual Needs

Children often forget to include the question when they first begin to create their own problems. Some children benefit from asking the question first, so that they don't forget it. Others may need to be prompted to give the facts and then prompted again for the question.

Some children may pose a question like one they just heard. They may repeat it exactly or perhaps include different numbers or slightly different items (for instance, a lion may become a tiger). This is fine and gives them the opportunity to experience the structure of the problem.

Working in pairs can support children who are still developing their language skills or who may be shy about suggesting new ideas.

REFERENCES/FURTHER READING

Cohen, Caron L. 2000. *How Many Fish?* New York: HarperCollins.
Quintero, Elizabeth, T. 2004. "Will I Lose a Tooth? Will I Learn to Read? Problem Posing with Multicultural Children's Literature." *Young*

A35–A37

Mathematical Focus

- Count to find one or two more.
- Count to find one or two less.
- Read numerals.

Potential Challenges and Misconceptions

Most young children do not recognize that finding one more than a certain number, say five, is the same as naming the next counting number, or six. Many adults are surprised when they first discover this aspect of children's thinking. This is because adults tend to underestimate the complex conceptual ideas related to counting and how much time these ideas take to form and solidify. Though initial counting activities stress the one-to-one correspondence between number names and numbers, understanding this association does not necessarily allow young children to infer that each number is one less than the next number or one more than the previous one. Even children who have some basic sense of this notion do not necessarily apply it to the solution of story problems or to find answers to questions such as *What is one more than three?*

One of the most basic addition fact strategies is to add one or two more by counting up, that is, saying one or two more number names. Thinking, *What do I add to four to get five?* also allows children to find 5 − 4 = 1. Some children are able to count backward from five to four for the same results. Such skills depend on understanding the relationship between number names and one or two more (or less) and being comfortable with counting up and down.

In the Classroom

Children usually enjoy playing games and play their favorite ones over and over. Providing practice with engaging activities is a wonderful way to give children the opportunities they need to gain expertise with numbers. *Climb the Towers* is one such activity. A spinner is provided on page A35 in the appendix. It shows the numerals 1 and 2 along with the associated number of dots. Use a brad to connect the needle to the face of the spinner. The boards for the game are on pages A36 and A37 in the appendix. The *Towers to Five* reproducible (page A36) has towers containing the numbers 1–5, and the *Towers to Ten* reproducible (page A37) has towers containing 1–10. You may want to introduce everyone to the simpler game first and then provide the larger towers as appropriate. Have children play in pairs, and give each player a game board and four game pieces or counters. Following are the directions for playing the game:

1. Each player places a game piece or counter below each tower on his or her game board.
2. Players take turns spinning and climbing up any one of their towers that number of spaces. Only one tower may be used in one turn.
3. If a player cannot complete a move using just one of his or her towers, then no move is taken and the turn ends.
4. The winner is the first player to move all his or her game pieces to the top floor (5 or 10) of the towers.

To help children attend to the numerical relationships embedded in the play, make statements about the moves of the game. For example, say, *I see you were on 4 and got a 1. Now you are on 5.* Encourage children to make predictions before they make their moves by summarizing the situations, for example, *Your spinner landed on 2. Which piece will you move? Where will it be after you move it?* After playing the game, tell the children to close their eyes and visualize a tower in their minds' eyes. Say, for instance, *You want to move your game piece that is on 3. You spin a 1. Where does the piece land?* When appropriate, you can ask, for example, *What is two more than two? What is one less than nine?*

Another activity you can use to help students practice counting up or back one or two is *What's in the Bag?* Working with a small group of children, invite a child to place four small cubes in an opaque bag. Once you have closed the bag, have the students confirm the number of cubes. Then add another cube and ask, *How many cubes are in the bag now?* Children then empty the bag to check their predictions. Use initial numbers as appropriate. You can add one or two cubes or, for more challenge, take one or two cubes away. Connect the actions to number sentences as appropriate.

Meeting Individual Needs

Climb the Towers can be adapted for a wide range of learners and to ensure that children are challenged at the right levels as they play. Variations include the following:

- Simplify the game by using smaller numbers. Make a single copy of the reproducible on page A35 and cut the towers to a height of three before making copies for the children.
- Encourage players to predict where their games pieces will land before moving them.
- Have students play the game in reverse: Players place all game pieces on the 10s (or 5s) and move down the towers until all the pieces are off. Or they can cover each numeral with a transparent disk and remove them top to bottom, to correspond to the spins.
- Allow a move of two to be split into two moves of one on different towers.
- Give players a spinner with the numerals 1, 2, and 3 or, if appropriate, one die.

REFERENCE/FURTHER READING

Griffin, Sharon. 2003. "Laying the Foundation for Computational Fluency in Early Childhood." *Teaching Children Mathematics* 9 (6): 306–9.

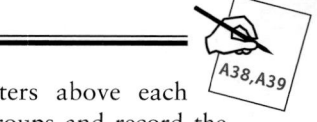

Mathematical Focus

- Practice addition and subtraction.
- Write number sentences for addition and subtraction.

Potential Challenges and Misconceptions

The Common Core State Standards for Mathematics expect kindergarten students to gain fluency when adding numbers that total five or when subtracting from five. Many students find it challenging to move from concrete to abstract representations of these relationships. We must expose prekindergartners to activities that allow them to practice combining and separating sets before fluency is required. Ideally, you should choose experiences that allow learners to participate on a variety of levels. For example, children can use real objects, fingers, drawings, or recall to find sums and differences. When teachers support diversity in the ways in which learners process information, they can use activities for wider ranges of age and readiness and can better ensure success in inclusive classrooms.

The standards also encourage, but don't require, children in kindergarten to write equations. It takes considerable time for young children to connect the actions of joining and separating to number sentences involving signs for addition, subtraction, and equality. Again, it is important that children have early exposure to activities that allow them to make connections among objects, actions, and symbolic notations.

In the Classroom

Number games and activities provide children with opportunities to practice their skills. They also allow learners with less developed verbal skills to occasionally develop their emerging mathematical ideas without struggling with the language of story problems. *Bean Toss* is an activity you can easily adapt to meet a variety of needs. To prepare for the game, write one number in each cup of an egg carton. For example, you might choose to randomly write the numerals *1–3* four times each, or the numerals *1–4* three times each, or the numbers *1–6* twice. One teacher keeps several *Bean Toss* egg cartons available for play. She has labeled the end of each carton with *1–3*, *1–4*, or *1–6* so that both the adults and the children can identify the difficulty levels at a glance.

Children play the game in pairs, alternating turns. Directions for the basic activity follow.

1. To begin a turn, one player places a bean in the egg carton and then closes the carton and shakes it.
2. Next the player opens the carton to see the number written on the cup where the bean landed and then gathers that many counters.
3. Then the player repeats the entire process once more.
4. Finally, he or she finds the total number of counters.
5. The children may play for an allocated amount of time or number of turns.

Explain the directions to a small group and demonstrate the game with a volunteer. Show the number sentence that corresponds to each turn and emphasize the meaning of the addition and equal signs. After the children understand the activity, pair them and give them an appropriately marked egg carton. Observe the children as they work. Look for learners who need assistance counting the items, who are able to subitize, and who are ready for more of a challenge.

Variations to the activity include the following:

- The children record numbers to represent each addend on the

They place the associated counters above each number. Then they join the two groups and record the sum after the equal sign.

- Younger pre-K children can just compare the number of counters from their first toss with the number from their second toss and tell which value is greater or less, or if they are equal.
- To add some competition, you can have each player take a turn and then see whose sum is greater.
- Children who are able to think more abstractly can toss two beans at once and use fingers, counting on, or recall to find the sum of the two numbers the beans land on.
- Cut an egg carton in half to create two six-cup shakers. Write the numerals *1*, *2*, and *3* twice (one number per cup) in one half and record the numerals *4*, *5*, and *6* twice in the cups of the other half. The student tosses one bean in each half. He or she gathers counters to represent the greater number, separates the number of beans indicated by the number that is less, and then finds the number of beans that are left. If you want the children to record number sentences for their work, give them copies of the *Bean Toss Subtraction* recording sheet on page A39 in the appendix.

Meeting Individual Needs

Young children develop number sense and fluency with addition and subtraction at different rates, and it is important to challenge all children regardless of their stage of understanding. For learners who need more support, it is helpful to provide five-frames or ten-frames for them to use with the counters. In addition to *Bean Toss*, games played with dotted dice also support a wide range of learners because children can count the dots or subitize to determine the number shown.

It is also important for us to remember that some young children progress easily to symbolic notation and are interested in its use. We need to provide for these learners as well. When Torin was five he had significant language and spatial skills. His teacher asked him to pick his favorite number less than ten. He chose eight right away, asking, "Did you know eight is a spider?"

His teacher was pleased that he was making a real-world connection to the number eight and responded, "Show me." She was surprised to discover that Torin was thinking of two connections (see figure). She had not noticed that a spider's body resembles the numeral 8.

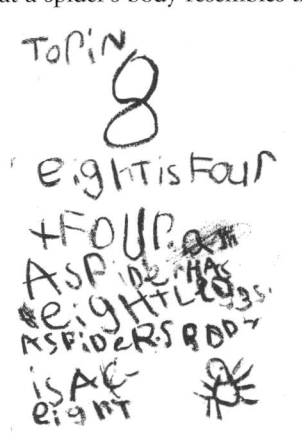

REFERENCE/FURTHER READING

National Governors Association (NGA) Center for Best Practices and Council of Chief State School Officers (CCSSO). 2010. *Common Core State*

FIVE-FRAMES

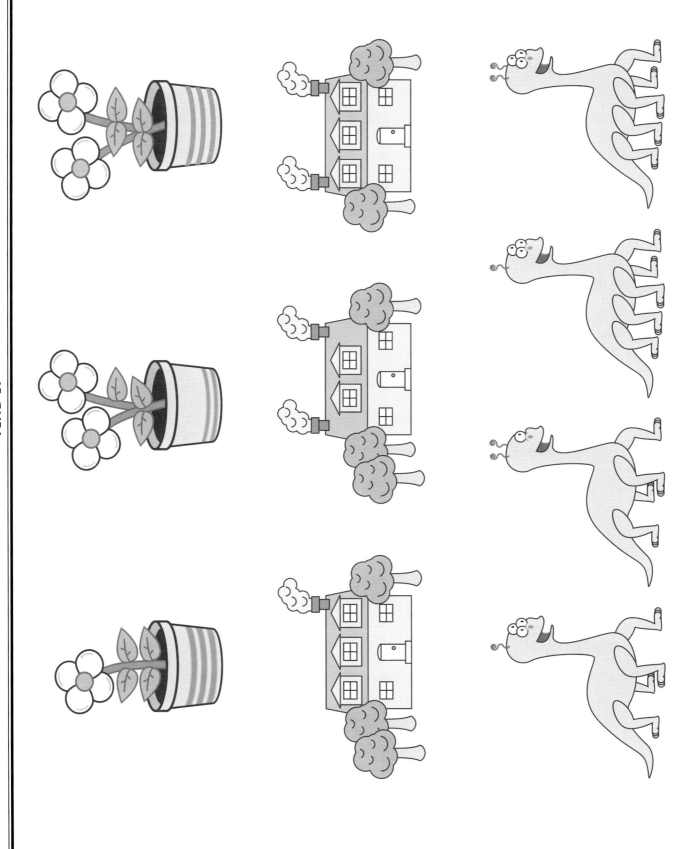

TEN-FRAMES

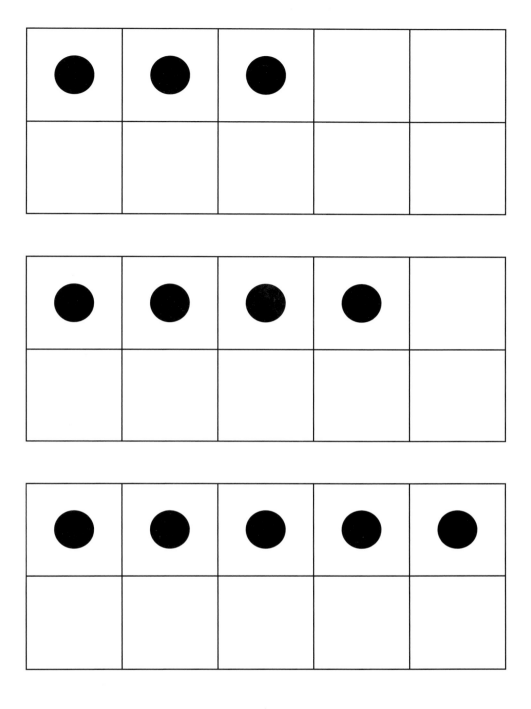

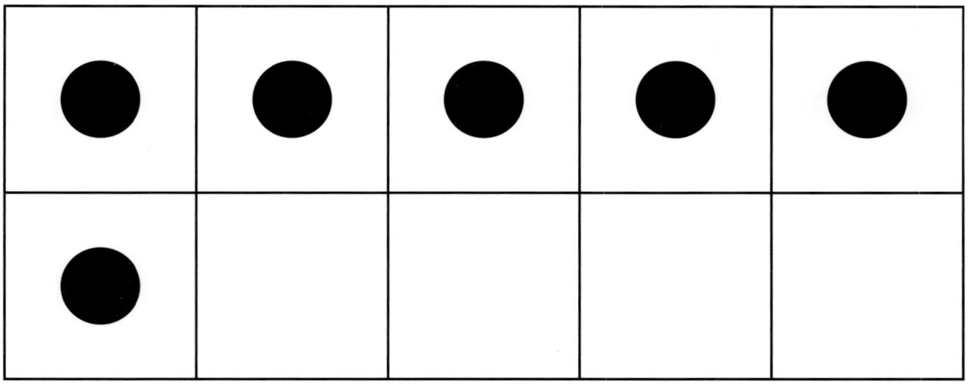

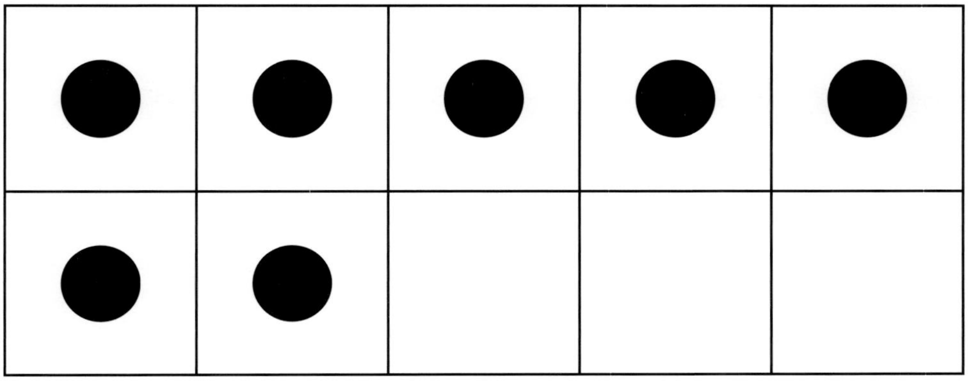

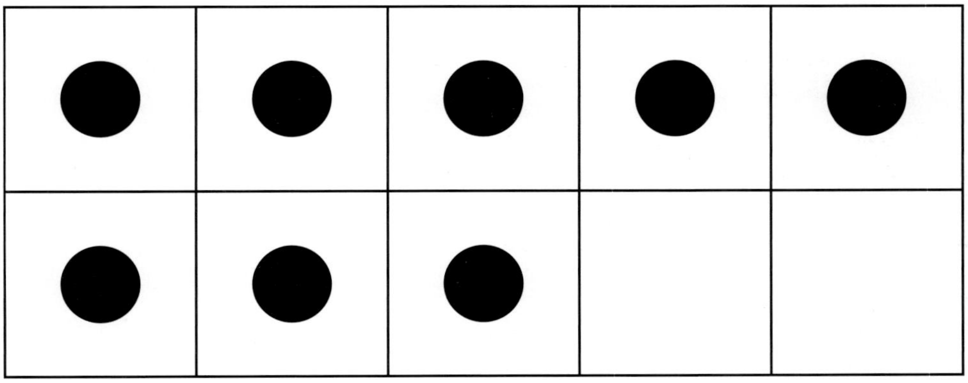

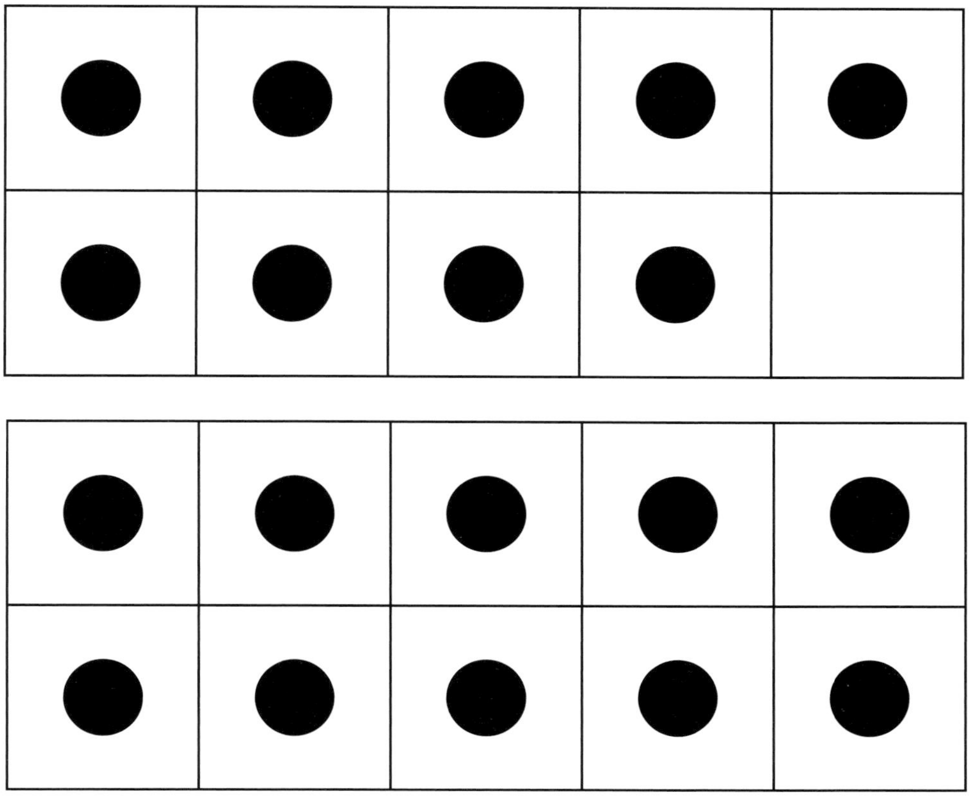

COUNTING ASSESSMENT FORM

Student's Name	Has demonstrated the ability to:			
	Say the number names in order up to:	Count sets accurately up to:	Match sets to symbols up to:	Write the numerals:

Zeroing in on Number and Operations: Key Ideas and Common Misconceptions, Grades Pre-K–K by Linda Dacey and Anne Collins. Copyright © 2011. Stenhouse Publishers.

Make copies of this reproducible on heavy stock. Cut out the puzzle pieces, and laminate them if possible. Give each child a set of the puzzle pieces.

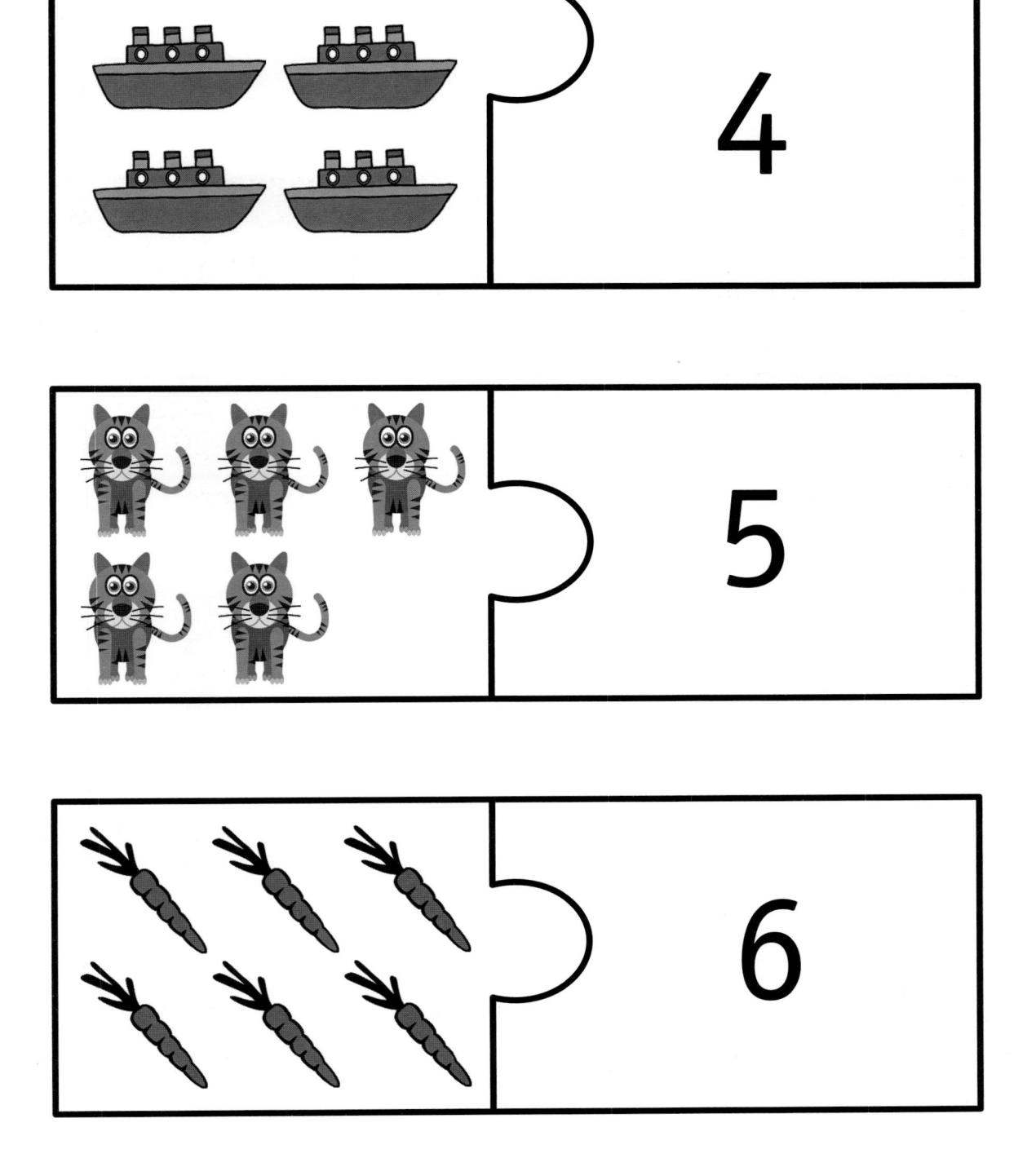

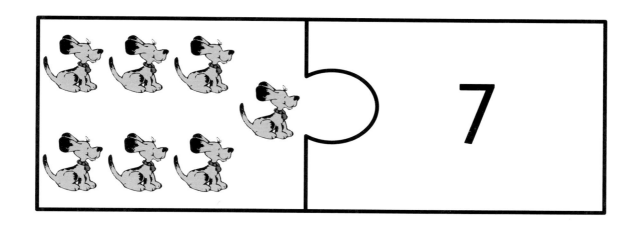

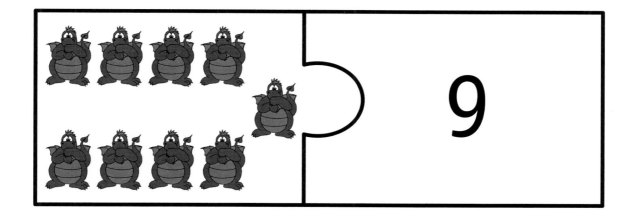

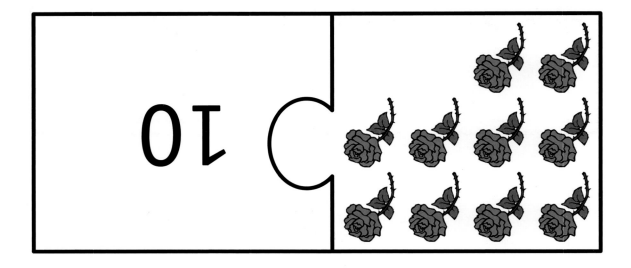

Make copies of this reproducible on heavy stock. Cut the cards in half, and laminate them if possible.

6

SIX

5

FIVE

4

FOUR

1

2

3

4

5

10

9

8

7

6

| 11 | 12 |

| 13 | 14 | 15 |

18	19	20

16	17

1	2	3	4
5	6	7	8
9		1	0

NUMBER STICKS

1	11	21	31	41
2	12	22	32	42
3	13	23	33	43
4	14	24	34	44
5	15	25	35	45
6	16	26	36	46
7	17	27	37	47
8	18	28	38	48
9	19	29	39	49
10	20	30	40	50

51	61	71	81	91
52	62	72	82	92
53	63	73	83	93
54	64	74	84	94
55	65	75	85	95
56	66	76	86	96
57	67	77	87	97
58	68	78	88	98
59	69	79	89	99
60	70	80	90	100

10	3	15	21	2
23	5	20	34	16
19	32	26	18	24
14	29	13	6	7
1	8	22	25	9
31	28	33	12	30
35	17	27	4	11

Name:

Write the letters of each bag.

_____ is more than _____

_____ is less than _____

_____ is the same as _____

Name:

Draw lines to show the matches.

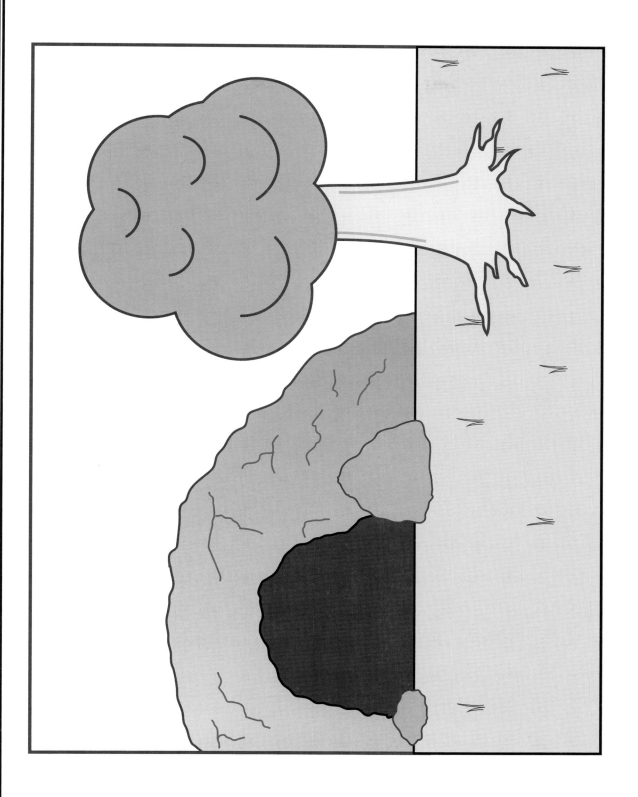

≠	≠
=	=
less	less
more	more

RELATIONSHIP CARDS

COMPARISON ASSESSMENT FORM

Student's Name:

Date:

Has demonstrated the ability to:

_____Use visual cues to compare the quantities of sets up to _____.

_____Use matching to compare the quantities of sets up to _____.

_____Use the order of number names to compare the quantities of sets up
to _____.

_____Use the terms *more, less,* and *same number as* to compare the quantities of sets
up to _____.

_____Use the terms *equal to* and *not equal to* to compare the quantities of sets up
to _____.

_____Write the symbols for *equal* and *not equal* to compare the quantities of sets.

_____Order more than two sets by quantity.

Date:

Has demonstrated the ability to:

_____Use visual cues to compare the quantities of sets up to _____.

_____Use matching to compare the quantities of sets up to _____.

_____Use the order of number names to compare the quantities of sets up
to _____.

_____Use the terms *more, less,* and *same number as* to compare the quantities of sets
up to _____.

_____Use the terms *equal to* and *not equal to* to compare the quantities of sets up
to _____.

_____Write the symbols for *equal* and *not equal* to compare the quantities of sets.

_____Order more than two sets by quantity.

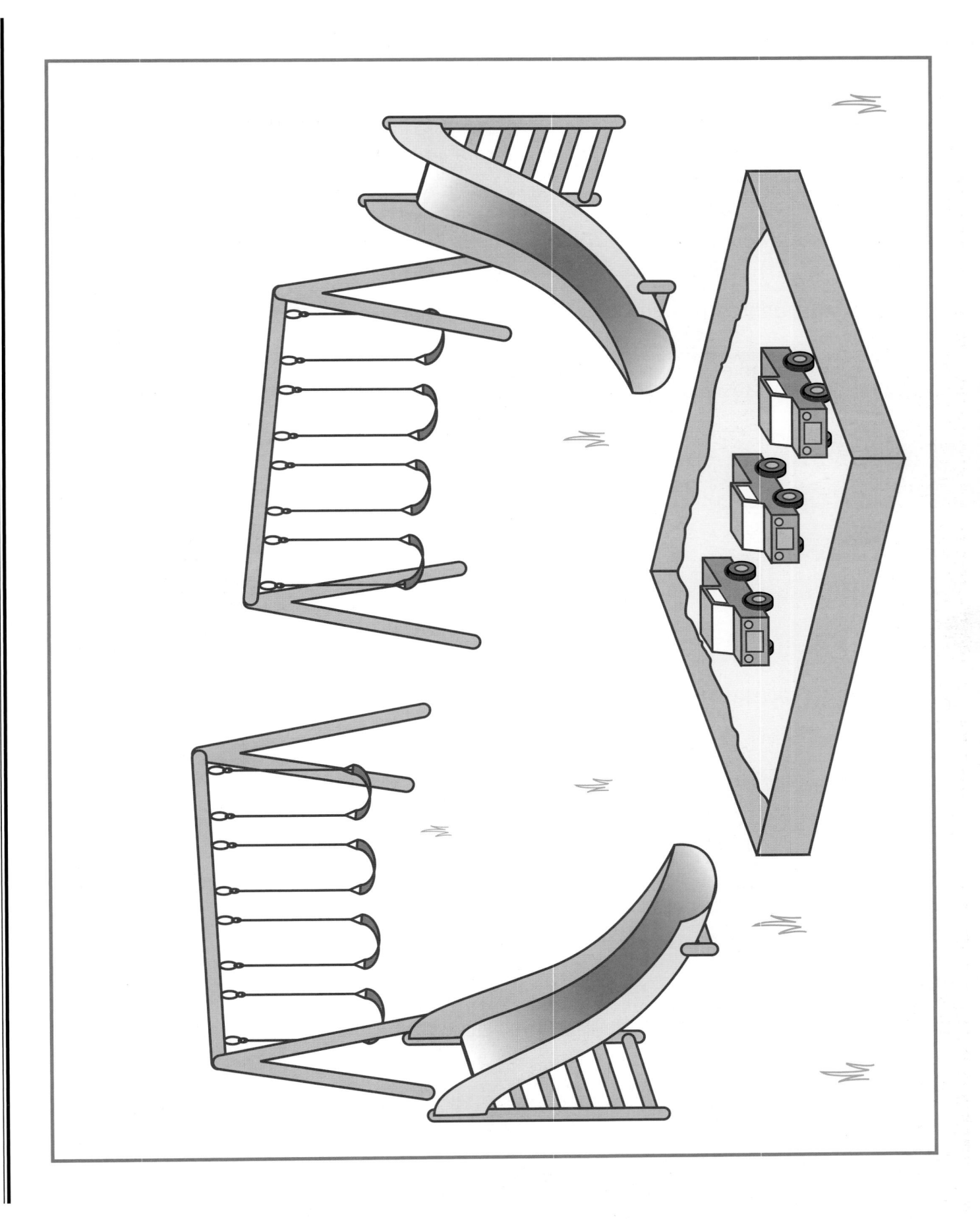

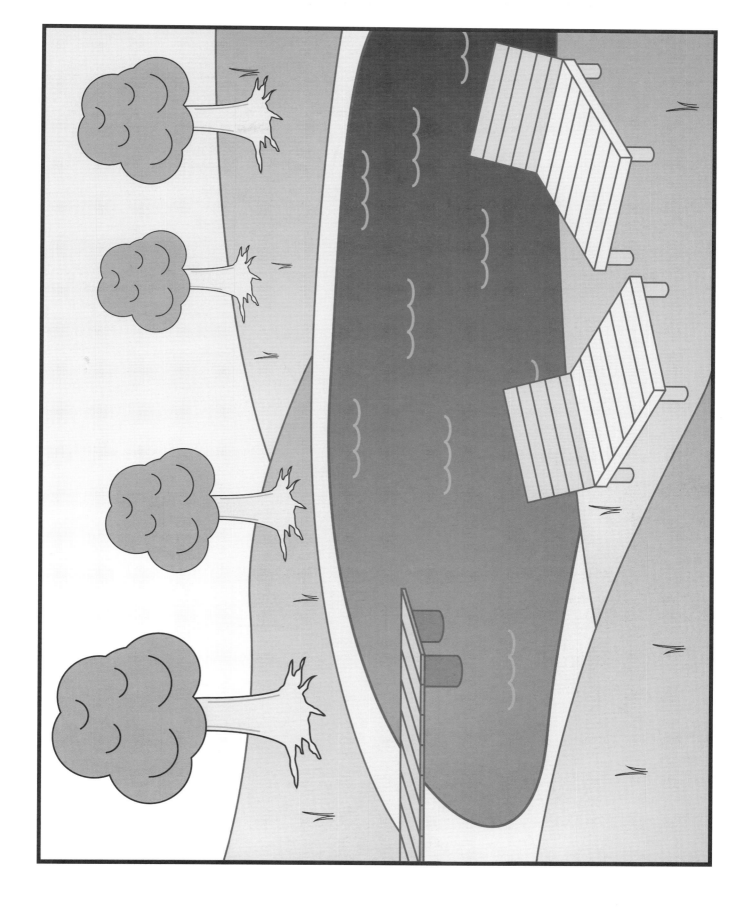

PATTERN BLOCK FILL-IN

Trace the blocks you use to fill the shapes. Fill in the blanks.

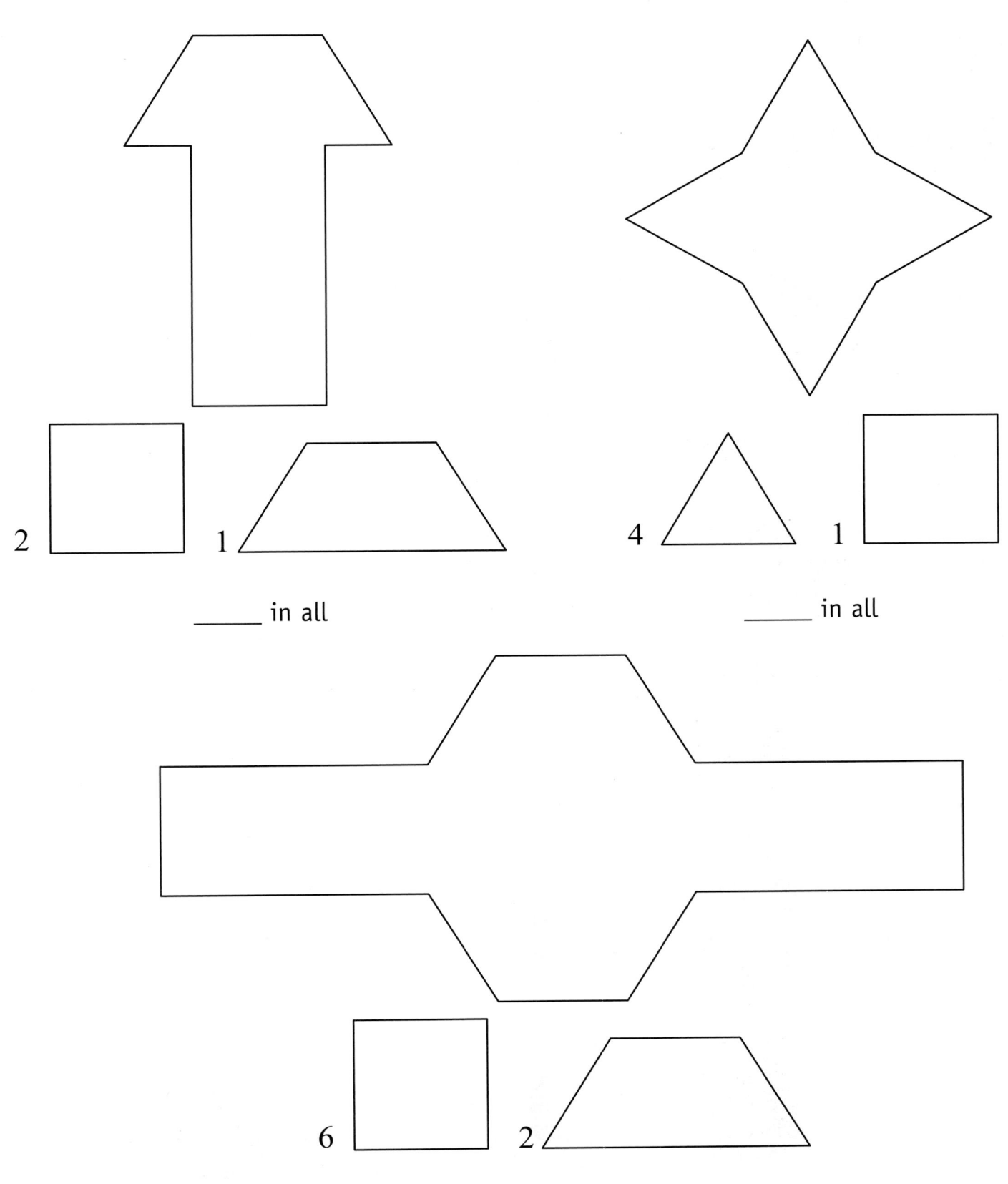

2 ☐ 1 ⬠

_____ in all

4 △ 1 ☐

_____ in all

6 ☐ 2 ⬠

_____ in all

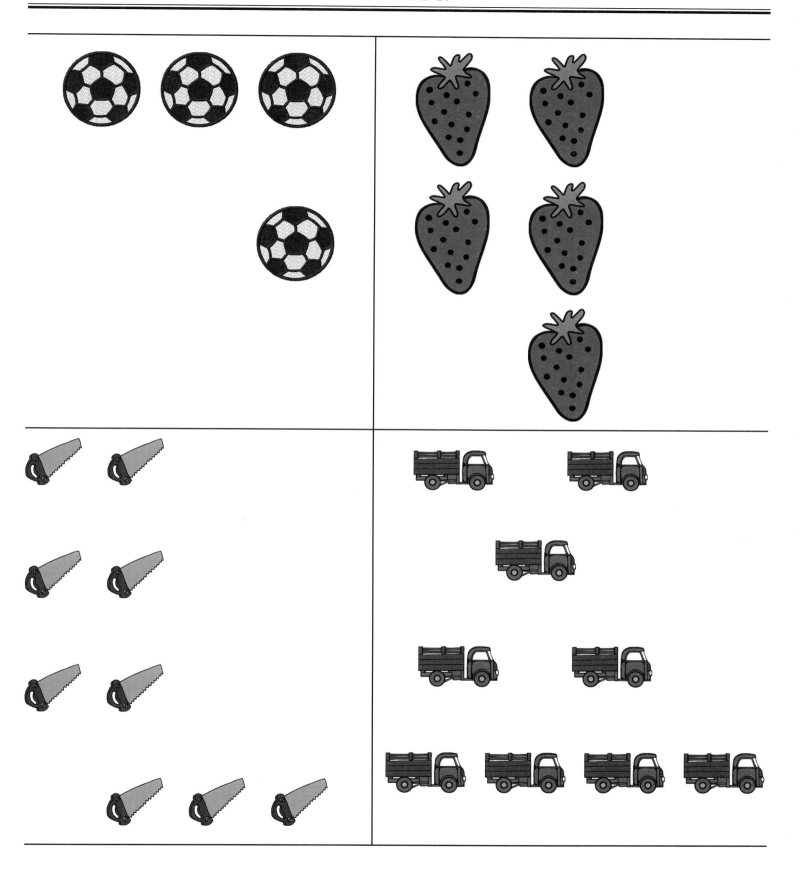

WHAT'S MISSING?

Name:

Draw the missing circles to match the number in each row.

4

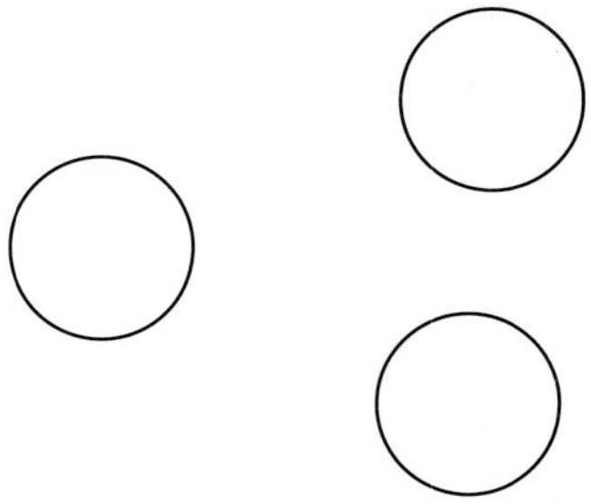

8

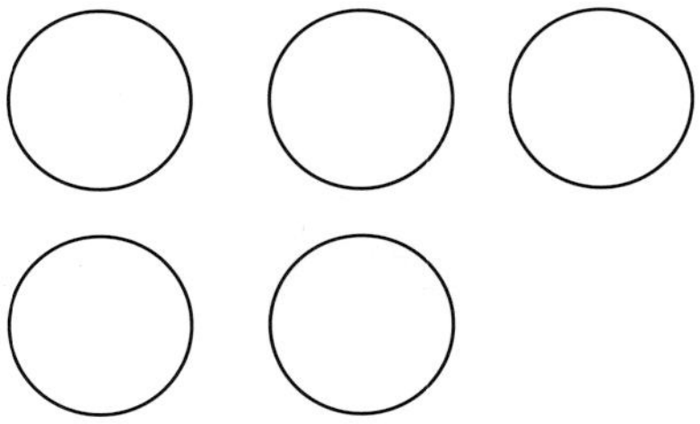

7

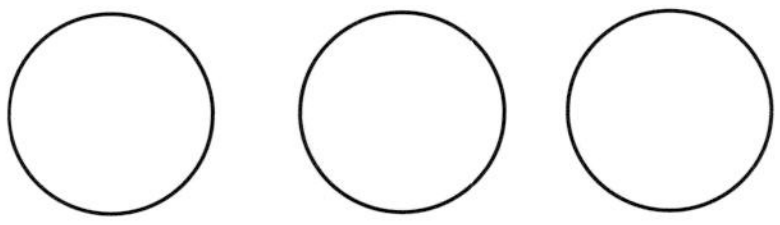

10

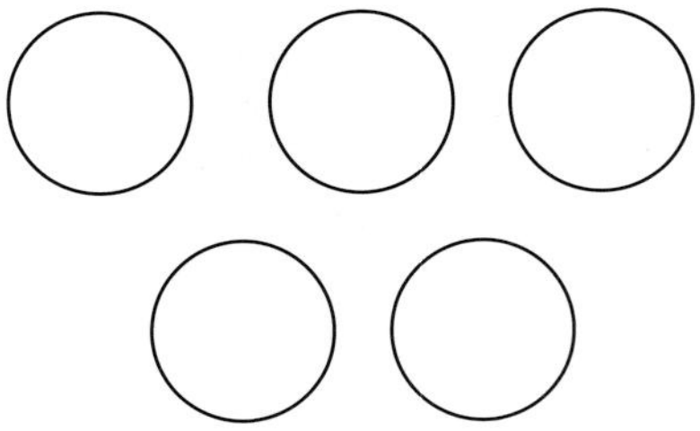

Name:

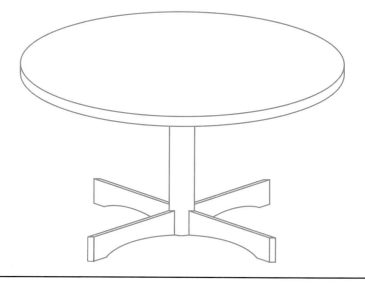

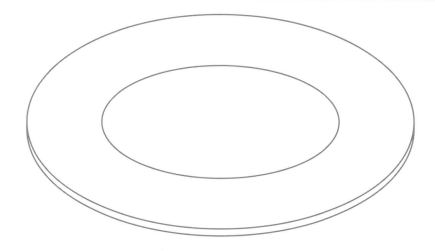

Problem 1 (addition)

There are four red pencils on the table. Dana puts one more pencil on the table. How many pencils are on the table now? (5)

Problem 1 (subtraction)

There are five pencils on the table. Dana takes one of the pencils. How many pencils are on the table now? (4)

Problem 2 (addition)

Brad saw three clowns sitting on the elephant. He also saw four clowns beside the elephant. How many clowns did Brad see in all? (7)

Problem 2 (subtraction)

There are seven clowns sitting on the elephant. Four of the clowns fall off the elephant. How many clowns are still on the elephant? (3)

Problem 3 (addition)

There are three red apples on the plate. Mr. Wilson puts three yellow apples there, too. How many apples are on the plate now? (6)

Problem 3 (subtraction)

There are six apples on the plate. Three of the apples are red. The rest of the apples are yellow. How many of the apples are yellow? (3)

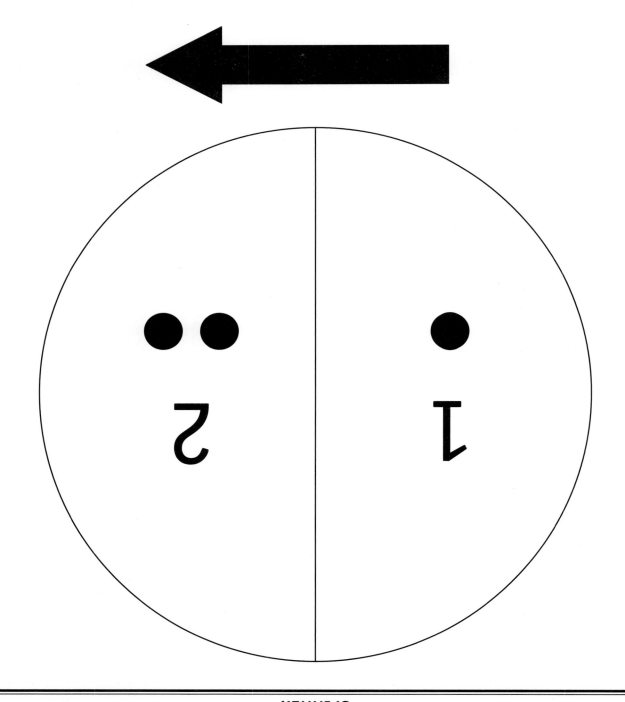

SPINNER

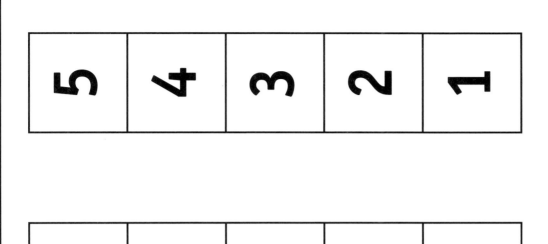

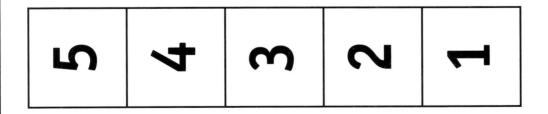

5	4	3	2	1

10	10	10	10
9	9	9	9
8	8	8	8
7	7	7	7
6	6	6	6
5	5	5	5
4	4	4	4
3	3	3	3
2	2	2	2
1	1	1	1

Zeroing in on Number and Operations: Key Ideas and Common Misconceptions, Grades Pre-K–K by Linda Dacey and Anne Collins. Copyright © 2011. Stenhouse Publishers.

Name:

Draw and write to show the numbers.

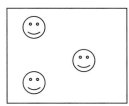 +  =

_____ 3 _____ + _____ 1 _____ = _____ 4 _____

 + [ ] = [ ]

_____ + _____ = _____

 + [ ] = [ ]

_____ + _____ = _____

BEAN TOSS SUBTRACTION

Name:

Draw and write to show the numbers.

$$\underline{\quad 5 \quad} - \underline{\quad 1 \quad} = \underline{\quad 4 \quad}$$

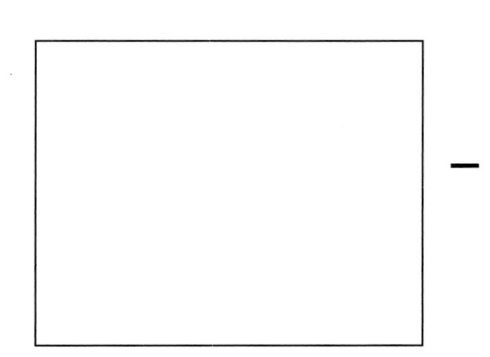  

— − — = —